Advocacy for Parents with Learning Difficulties

Developing advocacy support

The Joseph Rowntree Foundation has supported this project as part of its programme of research and innovative development projects, which it hopes will be of value to policy makers and practitioners. The facts presented and the views expressed in this report, however, are those of the authors and not necessarily those of the Foundation.

Advocacy for Parents
with Learning Difficulties

Developing advocacy support

Wendy Booth and Tim Booth

Pavilion

·

JR
JOSEPH
ROWNTREE
FOUNDATION

RESEARCH *INTO* PRACTICE

RESEARCH *INTO* PRACTICE

Advocacy for Parents with Learning Difficulties

Developing advocacy support

Wendy Booth and Tim Booth

Published by:

Pavilion Publishing (Brighton) Ltd.

8 St George's Place

Brighton

East Sussex BN1 4GB

Telephone: 01273 623222

Fax: 01273 625526

Email: pavpub@pavilion.co.uk

Website: www.pavpub.com

In association with:

The Joseph Rowntree Foundation

The Homestead

40 Water End

York YO3 6LP

First published 1998.

A catalogue record for this book is available from the British Library.

ISBN 1 900600 80 3

10 9 8 7 6 5 4 3 2 1

Editor: Liz Mandeville

Design and typesetting: Stanford Douglas

Illustrations: Richard Booth

Printing: York Publishing Services

Contents

Acknowledgements

We have reason to be grateful to the following people for their encouragement, advice and support in the course of this action project: Claire Benjamin, Diana Charles, Sue Dawson, Steve Dowson, Barbara Fletcher, and Ann Kilby. We were blessed by our fellow workers on Parents Together — Rita Hawley, Mick Rodgers and Jo Ryan — whose enthusiasm and commitment for the job exceeded the bounds of duty. Others we are unable to name — the parents who took part in the project and the practitioners who gave of their time — although our debt to them is enormous. Finally, our thanks go to the Joseph Rowntree Foundation for enabling us to put into practice ideas that have emerged from our earlier research in this field.

Chapter One

Introduction

This report…

- describes the work of **Parents Together**, an advocacy support project for parents with learning difficulties

- looks at the strengths and limitations of an advocacy approach to working with parents

- examines the lessons to be drawn from the project.

Parents Together was set up as an action research project with funding from the Joseph Rowntree Foundation. Its purpose was to work in partnership with parents to support them in ways that were:

- non-stigmatising

- non-intrusive

- responsive to the parents' own views of their needs.

The guiding aims of the project were to make parents feel better about themselves and better able to look after their children.

Parents Together ran for eighteen months from February 1996 to July 1997. This report combines both a start-to-finish account and an evaluation of the project. It can be read from cover to cover — as a story with overlapping plot-lines about being an advocate, doing advocacy, challenging the system and supporting parents — or it can be dipped into as a 'do-it-yourself' manual by those wanting to tread the same path. In this sense, the report is both a record of the **Parents Together** project and a source of reference for people working with parents who have learning difficulties or with other families needing advocacy support.

The project holds lessons for managers, policy-makers, practitioners, advocates and advocacy scheme co-ordinators. The report has something to say to all these readers:

- For managers and policy-makers, it shows how the absence of a basic infrastructure of supports geared to the needs of these families undermines their competence and leads to system abuse.

- For practitioners, it sets out guidance on good practice.

- For advocates, it illustrates the variety of roles that comprise the advocacy task, and the difficulties and compromises they bring.

- For advocacy scheme co-ordinators, it defines a set of principles endorsed by parents and shows how these can be put into practice.

Chapter Two
Why Parents with Learning Difficulties?

The number of parents with learning difficulties is unknown, though the numbers who are known to the health and welfare services are widely acknowledged to be rising steadily. The reasons for this trend are complex, and it is not easy to tell if more referrals really mean there are more parents. On the one hand, policies that reduce controls over the sexuality of people with learning difficulties might be expected to lead to more of them having children. The fact that increases in the number of parents have been reported in all countries which have moved towards services based on 'ordinary life' principles and community living would appear to support this interpretation.

On the other hand, families on the margins of competence might be finding it harder to manage in an increasingly competitive society. Greater intervention by the state in family life, closer surveillance of parents and their children and the widening of the child protection net may have brought more parents to the attention of the public services. Whatever the reasons for the apparent increase in families headed by a parent or parents with learning difficulties, they now represent a sizeable population whose special needs for education, training and support have so far not been adequately addressed by the health and social services.

Research has shown that parents with learning difficulties too often receive a raw deal from the statutory services. The evidence points to high rates (40–60%) for the removal of children from the family home, but low investment in the kinds of service and support that might enable them to bring up their children. Current work with such families is characterised by several features that serve to enhance their vulnerability and test their resourcefulness:

- **The presumption of incompetence** — or the belief that parents' innate limitations make them unfitted for parenthood.

> **Parents Together** viewed parents as people with problems, not as the problem themselves.

- **A deficiency perspective** — or a tendency always to focus on people's deficits and on what they cannot do.

> **Parents Together** put the emphasis on people's positive qualities, and sought to build on their abilities and strengths.

- **System abuse** — meaning policies and practices that harm the families they are supposed to support or protect.

> **Parents Together** set out to provide independent advocacy support to parents in their dealings with practitioners and the services.

- **Competence-inhibiting support** — meaning support that de-skills parents, reinforces their feelings of inadequacy and undermines their independence.

  Parents Together aimed at all times to allow parents to feel in control, to encourage them to handle their own problems and to create opportunities for them to demonstrate their competence.

- **Top-down priorities** — meaning that the professional as trained expert is usually in control and running the show.

  Parents Together worked in partnership with parents and gave priority to parents' views of their own needs.

- **A child-centred focus** — the primary focus of attention for practitioners is usually the welfare of the children.

  Parents Together treated the family as a unit, and recognised that parents have needs as people, too.

- **Blaming the victim** — family and child-care problems are often ascribed to the limitations of the parents when they owe more to environmental pressures or deficiencies in the support services.

  Parents Together aimed to work with parents to reduce the external pressures on the family that make their parenting more difficult.

- **Crisis-driven services** — families often have to wait until a crisis erupts before the services will respond.

  Parents Together tried to head off problems or prevent them blowing up into a crisis, by maintaining close involvement with the families.

- **Lack of trust** — many parents have had bad experiences of the services in the past and are often reluctant to seek help, even when they need it, for fear of where it might lead.

  Parents Together regarded the formation of positive, non-threatening, trusting relationships with parents as a primary goal.

- **High drop-out rates** — keeping families interested and involved in early intervention programmes, parenting training programmes, support groups and the like is a recurring problem.

  Parents Together aimed to motivate parents by offering support in a way, and at a pace, that was right for them.

Chapter Three
A Model of Support

Parents Together was based on an explicit model of parenting and social support.

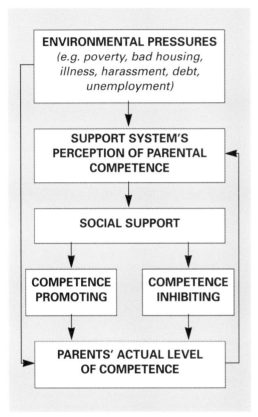

In this model, **parental competence** is influenced by the **environmental pressures** bearing on the family and the **social support** the family receives.

Environmental pressures exert both a direct effect on the parenting load, and hence the parents' ability to cope, and an indirect effect by influencing how well they are seen to be coping, and hence the type and level of support they need.

Social support impacts on parental competence for better or worse, depending on whether it promotes or inhibits the parents' capacity to manage the parental task.

The parents' **actual level of competence** in turn feeds back to reinforce how they are perceived by the support system.

> Put simply, the message of the model is: Give people better lives and they'll become better parents.

Drawing on this model, **Parents Together** set out to enhance parental competence in three ways:

- by reducing the environmental pressures on parents that undermine their ability to cope

- by challenging discriminatory views of their fitness for parenthood, their ability to learn and acquire new skills, or their capacity for love and affection

- by supporting parents in ways that improve their confidence and encourage their sense of self-worth.

Chapter Four
A Principled Approach

Parents Together adopted a principled approach to working in partnership with parents, drawing on the precedents and examples set by:

- **the self-advocacy movement** — especially the idea of people working together to find their own voice, speak up for themselves, challenge the identity they have been assigned and fight for their rights as full citizens

- **the citizen advocacy movement** — especially the idea of actively representing the interests of people (in this case, parents) with learning difficulties and helping them establish informal supports within their neighbourhoods

- **the self-help movement** — especially the idea of people joining together to do something about their common problems and to enhance their sense of personal identity.

Parents' involvement in the project was voluntary. All information received or shared was regarded as confidential (following the example of the Samaritans). All workers on the project had to be parents themselves (following the example of Home-Start and Parentline groups).

Chapter Five
Principles in Practice

In deciding how to put these principles into practice, **Parents Together** drew heavily on the lessons and experience of supported parenting programmes in the USA (a list of useful references is given in *Appendix 1*). A set of guidelines for workers on the project was drawn up as a starting point:

Parents Together is a support network for people with learning difficulties and their partners who are mums and dads, expectant parents, or thinking about having a baby. It is open to couples where one or both partners have learning difficulties, single parents with learning difficulties, parents who have had children taken into care, parents with dependent children, and parents whose children have left home.

- Parents' involvement in the project is voluntary. ('No-one can make you let me into your home, no-one can make you come to group meetings.')

- Our purpose is to help people do things for themselves, not to do things for them.

- When we withdraw, families must be stronger as a result of our involvement, not more dependent.

- Beware of stereotyping and preconceived ideas.

- Focus on building a family's strengths rather than concentrating on its weaknesses.

- Parents are a resource, not a problem.

Remember

Supporting parents supports children.

- Always respect the family home.

- Never underestimate parents.

- Parents know if you don't like them. Own up to the project co-ordinator about your feelings, and be prepared to make way for someone else.

- Beware of imposing your values on parents.

- Do not undermine parents in their handling of their own children.

Remember

Advocacy is the guiding principle in all dealings with parents.

- **Parents Together** does not operate a policy of obligatory reporting. Any worries or suspicions should be discussed with the parents first, and if necessary thereafter with the project co-ordinators.

- The project will operate a policy of open records and parents will be given a copy of everything written about them.

- Mums and dads are people, too, whose needs as adults must be recognised, as well as their responsibilities as parents.

- Be truthful about who you are. **Parents Together** is a project based at the university and not a bunch of people doing work out of the goodness of their hearts.

> **Remember**
> No dealing behind parents' backs.

- Parents must be assured that the project has no connection with the statutory services and our actions must never compromise this independence.

> **Remember**
> **Parents Together** is not seeking to replicate or replace the work of practitioners. The advocacy role is about making sure parents receive the support and services to which they are entitled.

- Parents are best supported in the context of their own extended families, neighbourhoods and communities. Stimulate and build on existing circles of support, with the parents' consent.

- Parents must be engaged as active partners in all aspects of the project.

- Parents should be enabled to feel in control and to experience being competent.

> **Remember**
> At all times the project should aim at:

- **enabling** parents by creating opportunities for them to exhibit their competence

- **empowering** parents by improving their sense of control over their own lives

- **enhancing** parents' self-esteem

- **extending** parents' social networks.

Chapter Six
The Action Project

As an action project, **Parents Together** operated on two fronts:

- **running support groups** — bringing together parents in order to share their experiences, to learn from and support each other, to reduce isolation and loneliness, to combat stress, to encourage strengths and abilities, and to enhance self-esteem.

- **outreach work** — developing the trust of parents new to the project, getting to know the parents better, maintaining contact with parents unable to attend the support groups, helping to mobilise community supports, accompanying parents to appointments with social workers, housing officials, schools, solicitors etc., and offering personal support, mostly in parents' homes.

Other activities providing a bridge between these two parts of the project included:

- **crisis advocacy** — for parents and families facing immediate problems that threaten to overwhelm them

- **a telephone helpline** — for people wanting a worker to call, to cancel a visit, to off-load, a bit of advice or just to chat.

- **parent-to-parent links** — bringing together parents for friendship or mutual support

- **a resource network** — offering information and guidance on sources of practical help.

The project team employed on **Parents Together** was made up of four workers:

Wendy Booth was Director of the project. She had been working as a researcher with parents who have learning difficulties for five years, and also had five years experience as adviser to a self-advocacy group.

Rita Hawley was engaged as a half-time development worker for the full eighteen months of the action project. Rita brought with her experience of working with families on low incomes.

Jo Ryan was employed one day a week for one year. She had worked in special needs education and was experienced in teaching adults with learning difficulties. Jo's sister is also a parent with learning difficulties.

Mick Rodgers worked on the project one day a week for a year. He also worked for a community health programme for people with learning difficulties. Mick's mother had learning difficulties.

Who was involved

There were 25 families involved in **Parents Together** between February 1996 and July 1997:

- eight families joined the project in the first three months and remained through to the end

- ten families left the project before the completion of the action phase

- fifteen families were still involved in the project when it came to an end.

A further 12 families were known of by project workers. Practical limits on the advocacy load prevented these families from being invited to join **Parents Together**.

Initially, most parents were contacted through the health and social services. When the project was up and running, however, other means of getting in touch opened up, and the names of families were given to us by, for example, solicitors and voluntary organisations. Some parents were brought along by those already in the project. **Parents Together** did not take referrals from practitioners. We were happy for them to put us in touch with people who might like to join, but membership was voluntary and only for parents who wanted to take part. In other words, joining the project was a decision for parents, not for practitioners as referral agents.

> **A practical rule of thumb:**
> Experience on the project suggests that eight families is the upper limit for a full-time advocate.

These twenty-five families included twenty-three mothers with learning difficulties, three fathers with learning difficulties, two (single) mothers without learning difficulties, and ten fathers without learning difficulties. The two mothers without learning difficulties were introduced by other parents to the support groups. They shared the same problems of isolation, powerlessness and vulnerability as the other parents. They did not receive outreach support.

Among the twenty-five families, there were six married couples, seven cohabiting partnerships, seven single mothers, four divorced/ separated mothers, and one mother who was living with two men.

Nineteen families in the project had between them thirty-five children living at home. These children ranged in age from 0 to 24 years; 29 were under 11 and the remainder were older. A mother and five couples had no children at home with them. During the course of the project, two more babies were born, three mothers became pregnant, and one child was taken into care.

In addition, eighteen children from these families had been fostered or adopted, three (now adult) children were living independently, six children were living with an ex-partner and two children had died.

There were three grandmothers with learning difficulties among the parents in the project.

Only two out of the twenty-five families owned their own house. Most (20) were council tenants. Two single mums lived with their own parents. During the course of the project, eight families moved house at least once. Ten were waiting to move.

All the parents in the project were unemployed. Fifteen had a phone. Five ran a car.

All but two of the families were receiving some form of support from statutory sources when they joined the project; thirteen families were receiving three or more supports. All families were receiving support at the time they left the project or when it ended.

Contact with parents

Conveying something of the extent of involvement with families is not easy. Contact with some families was greater than with others. People's needs shaped the frequency of their contact with their advocate. The length of home visits varied. The work done on behalf of families cannot be measured by the time spent with them.

Crudely, then, the blunt figures on the frequency of communication between the families and project workers are:

- 653 contact meetings (including visits and support group sessions)
- 212 phone calls to parents from advocates
- 193 phone calls to advocates from parents
- 14 letters to parents
- one letter from a parent.

Being responsive to parents' views of their own needs meant some made greater use of **Parents Together** than others. For example, one mother was visited 61 times, attended the support group 58 times and rang her advocate 48 times. By contrast, another mother, who was in the project for a similar length of time, was visited just 22 times, attended the support group once, and phoned her advocate once (as she was on the phone, her advocate was able to ring her — 39 times — to keep in contact).

Parents were not left stranded at the end of the project. Prior to its ending, the advocates began to work with the parents to determine how appropriate support, if needed, could be sustained after they withdrew. A plan was drawn up with every parent, setting out their views of their short- and longer-term needs and the possible ways in which these might be met. Parents were given a copy of their plan (see *Appendix 2* for a sample). All the shorter-term needs of parents were addressed before the advocate withdrew — either with supports being put in place or with a source of support being located. Possible ways of meeting the parents' longer-term needs were also identified, and the parents were advised on how to follow them up. The only thing requested by parents for which it was not possible to find a substitute was their advocate.

Chapter Seven
Advocacy in Action

This chapter describes the advocacy work undertaken with parents as part of the project, highlights the lessons it holds for practice, and pinpoints some of the difficulties and compromises encountered when adopting an advocacy approach to supporting parents.

At one time or another, sometimes simultaneously, the following roles have come to the fore when working with parents:

- the advocate as witness
- the advocate as buffer
- the advocate as voice
- the advocate as go-between
- the advocate as interpreter
- the advocate as listener
- the advocate as scribe
- the advocate as problem-solver
- the advocate as fixer
- the advocate as conduit
- the advocate as sounding-board
- the advocate as confidante
- the advocate as ally
- the advocate as sleuth
- the advocate as mentor
- the advocate as observer
- the advocate as mover and shaker.

Advocate as witness...

'It helped having her there.'

means...

sometimes simply being there is enough. 'Being there' is not about acting for parents, but about lending them authority. Even this passive support empowers people and makes them feel that they can get things done. Knowing there is someone there watching what they are doing also helps to keep officials and practitioners on their toes, and deters them from taking advantage of people who are often seen as unable to fight back.

Moira Potter wanted to open a bank account to help her save money towards a holiday. The bank required her to produce an ID. She had tried twice to get a National Insurance card from the local DSS office but had been refused. An advocate accompanied her on her third visit and, when Moira asked again, a

regulation form was handed over and
a card was finally issued.

Irene Sharman lived in a large block of
flats and suffered daily harassment from
kids. After they'd broken off her front-
door handle, she went to the housing
office and asked for it to be mended as
soon as possible because her house
wasn't secure. She was told it would take
a week. Later that day she called in again
with her advocate and made the same
request. A new door handle was fixed
within half an hour.

Other situations in which the advocate acted
as witness:

- meetings at school with teachers
- interviews with housing officials
- needs assessments and individual
  planning sessions
- statutory review meetings
- case conferences
- police interviews.

Practice points

- Helping parents to be independent means
  they need to keep control of what is
  happening. When an advocate
  accompanies a parent, it is important for
  the parent to make the enquiry or voice
  the complaint first. Only if the parent
  becomes flustered or the official is being
  unclear or uncooperative should the
  advocate intervene and back up what the
  parent has been saying.

- Avoid the official's gaze. Officials will often
  try to channel their remarks through the
  advocate. Avoid this by not catching their
  eye and by looking at the parent.

Difficulties and compromises

- So much of what needed to be done to
  sort out people's problems necessarily
  took place over the phone. Simple
  practicalities made public phones too
  difficult to use for this purpose. The
  advocate would often have to make calls
  for parents who had no phone of their
  own and then relay back the outcome.
  This practice did not encourage
  independence.

Advocate as buffer...

'*It takes a load off our shoulders.*'

means...

helping to absorb some of the pressures on
the family by fielding or deflecting matters
that might exacerbate their troubles or stress.

After experiencing victimisation by
neighbours, Eric and Emily Burgess and
their two sons were re-housed at the
rough end of another large, low-income
estate. Before long, they again became
the target of a campaign of vandalism by
gangs of local kids. When local authority
officials threatened to take action against
them over the state of the house, their
advocate suggested that Eric and Emily
give them her telephone number as the
person acting on behalf of the family in

this matter. Eric and Emily accepted this offer. The advocate was able to put the onus back on the local authority by pointing out its responsibilities as landlord to tenants facing victimisation by neighbours. She was also able to explain the family's fear of retribution to the police when they contacted her about Eric's refusal to name their attackers.

Olive Robinson and her partner, Grant, had their only child taken into care on suspicion of non-accidental injury. The parents were given three contact sessions a week, the main one being on a Monday. They were upset when they had to miss a session on Easter Monday because no-one was available to supervise on a bank holiday. With two more bank holidays coming up, the advocate anticipated that arrangements needed to be reviewed to avoid further distress. She was able to negotiate contact time on other days.

Other examples of advocate as buffer:

- fending off punitive action by a school over a child's non-attendance

- deflecting accusations of inadequate parenting back on to the local authority for its failure to deliver promised support to a family

- pacifying neighbours threatening to report a mother for the state of her house

- protecting a mother from her irate partner's efforts to trace her after she moved out.

Practice points

- In dealing with families whose lifestyle one would not necessarily seek to defend,

it is important to remember that the role of the advocate is to understand rather than to judge.

- Be ready to assume responsibility when things don't turn out as planned ('I should have seen it wouldn't work'), where doing so might preserve a parent's self-esteem.

Difficulties and compromises

- Parents were sometimes unwilling to pursue legitimate complaints against people in authority for fear of bringing more trouble on themselves. The advocate had to respect their feelings even when her own instincts were otherwise. She wasn't in a position to protect the family against any comeback.

- Sometimes parents' problems arose from the behaviour of adult sons or daughters still living in the family home. Trying to change their behaviour was not the role of the advocate.

Advocate as voice...

'She helped me to ask questions at meetings.'

means...

making sure the parents' side of the story is represented and their views are heard.

> Olive Robinson, a mother with learning difficulties, and her partner were involved in care proceedings and had to attend a succession of core group meetings, case conferences, statutory reviews, assessment sessions, and court appearances. Their advocate went with them to all these meetings and helped by explaining the procedures, speaking up for Mrs Robinson when she became agitated or distressed, and ensuring that her point of view, as well as her partner's, was not overlooked because of her lack of fluency, poor recall, and understandable reticence in intimidating circumstances.

> Alice Sykes had already had one child adopted and was living in a mother and baby unit with her second son. A case conference was called to decide whether the child should be placed on the Child Protection Register. Seven professionals were ranged round the table to give their reports on Alice and her baby. The advocate was able to support Alice in speaking up for herself at the meeting, talk through the options that had been offered to her by the chairperson, and help her explain to the professionals the reasons for her choice.

Other examples of advocate as voice:

- ensuring parents got their views and opinions across at assessments and children's reviews at school

- supporting a parent in choosing the style of her surgical shoes, instead of having the specialist foist his choice on her as had happened in the past

- helping parents communicate their worries about their own or their children's health to GPs and hospital specialists

- enabling a mother to express her desire for more involvement in her fostered son's education, as a result of which she started attending parents' evenings and was sent copies of his school reports

- giving evidence at an inquest on behalf of a family.

Practice points

- Case conferences and review meetings were always fraught occasions for parents. A key role of the advocate at these times was to make sure the parents understood the form and purpose of the meetings.

- Parents' deficits and shortcomings are usually quickly picked up and pointed out, unlike system failures. The advocate should remind service providers about their promises, especially when agreed supports are taking a long time to set up, and ensure they keep to their side of the bargain.

- All letters written on parents' behalf were composed with them, and read back to ensure they said what the parents wanted to say. Where parents wanted an advocate to speak for them, what should be said was always agreed with them beforehand.

- Parents may need to be advised what questions to ask in order to obtain the information they want.

- Find reasons for saying good things about the parents.

Difficulties and compromises

- Speaking up does not mean talking for parents. Sometimes advocates must bite their tongue. When a male member of staff at a day centre refused permission for a female colleague to accompany a mother to report her rape to the police, the mother decided not to complain about his intervention, in case she jeopardised her place at the centre. However much the advocate felt the staff member should have been reported, the parent had to have the final word.

- The advocate must be wary of assuming that other people in the family circle (such as a spouse, partner, grandparent or older child) speak for the parent with learning difficulties. Equally, in trying to engage directly with the parent with learning difficulties, the advocate must make sure these others don't feel ostracised and that the advocacy relationship doesn't cause damaging arguments at home.

- Advocates must beware of encouraging practitioners to communicate with parents through them and of undermining parents by giving the impression that practitioners will only listen when the advocate does the talking.

Advocate as go-between...

'She talked to my dad, explaining things to him.'

means...

helping to facilitate and improve liaison between the family, practitioners and the services.

Eric and Emily Burgess applied for a housing transfer after four years of living in fear of their neighbours who had subjected them to a campaign of intimidation and harassment. Before accepting their case for priority, a housing official called to inspect the condition of their property. After looking the place over, he took their advocate to one side and confided that he intended to report the house as having been unsatisfactorily maintained. As evidence, he cited a bucket of urine he'd seen on the landing. The advocate pointed out that the Burgess' bathroom was down-stairs, and that it had once been common practice to keep a chamber pot under the bed. She also offered to let him have a detailed account of the victimisation the family had suffered and how it had brought them down. The official agreed to fill in the form 'conditionally' pending this information. The Burgesses and their advocate put together a letter docu-menting the family's experiences and included a date-stamped photograph of their living room, newly decorated, taken shortly after they had moved in. When housing arranged another visit to assess any liability for repairs, the advocate advised the Burgesses to prepare for it as best they could, given that every window except one had been broken and boarded up. The family were smartly turned out and the house tidy when the official arrived.

Julie Bennett was a single parent with three children under five, the youngest of whom had sickle-cell anaemia. She herself suffered from epilepsy and post-natal depression. Ms Bennett had no support from either her family or professionals. The last time her health visitor called she was so glad to see her she'd burst into tears. Since then, the health visitor had not been back and Julie blamed herself. An advocate was able to re-establish links with the health visitor and to arrange a regular schedule of visits.

Other examples of advocate as go-between:

- mediating with private landlords

- liaison between parents and neighbours when grievances arose between them

- explaining court procedures to grandparents involved in care proceedings

- reporting harassment to the housing office

- acting as an intermediary between parents and other family members

- translating the outcomes and decisions of case conferences and reviews into language the parents could understand

- providing a point of contact between parents and their solicitors

- ensuring as necessary that practitioners know what others involved in a family are doing (a crucial task where families are involved with a large number of practitioners; in one case, a family was seeing two social workers, a health visitor, a midwife, two support workers, a psychologist and a community nurse, on a weekly basis).

Practice points

- An advocate could often assist parents by making a list of the things they wanted to ask or say at a review. The parents could then choose either to speak or just to hand over the list — or neither.

- Conflicting advice from different practitioners was a common problem for parents. The advocate was able to refer mixed messages back to their source for clarification.

- A good part of an advocate's time is taken up working behind the scenes, making phone calls, writing letters, finding out information, or chasing up practitioners. The parents' permission must always be obtained before assuming this role, and they must be kept informed of the outcome.

- Advocacy is about knowing when to act for someone and when to enable them to act for themselves, and striking the right balance between the two.

- Advocates should work to educate practitioners about the parents.

- Don't make any assumptions about a family based on information from official sources.

- Remember that the parents' interests come first when dealing with professionals and agencies on their behalf. Always think about how your actions might rebound on them.

- Ensure that parents receive copies of any written documentation due to them, such as the minutes of case conferences they have attended or LEA statements on their children.

- See that parents know where their support worker is based, who employs her, what she is supposed to do for the family, her hours of work and where her supervisor can be contacted.

Difficulties and compromises

- The advocate had to be wary of co-option — of being drawn into talking about parents and their families with professionals rather than talking to professionals on behalf of parents.

- Activating others (parents or practitioners) to do something often took longer and called for more time and effort than doing it oneself.

- Practitioners who failed to understand the role of advocate sometimes showed hostility or refused to accept that the advocate was acting for the parents.

- Advocates experienced the same frustration as parents when practitioners gave them wrong or incomplete information or failed to return phone calls, answer letters, honour appointments or do as they promised.

- Advocates sometimes found it hard not to let their own feelings about the treatment meted out to parents influence their relationships with practitioners.

Advocate as interpreter...

'She explains to me what I don't understand.'

means…

translating officialese into language the parents can understand, explaining procedures and otherwise making information accessible to them.

> Ruby Mason had been sexually and physically abused as a child by her father. She'd also had her first son adopted and a daughter die from meningitis. These were painful memories. Her remaining four children were all in foster care, and she was due to attend a court hearing to decide their future. In the meantime, she was obliged to take part in a series of assessments. Ruby's advocate went along, at her request, and was able to explain to her in simple terms the questions she found difficult to understand. At one point, she was asked about her family background and became very distressed. In the end, Ruby only agreed to continue with the assessment if the advocate was allowed to ask the questions. The social workers consented to her request.
>
> Ruby had difficulty grasping the purpose of the child-care proceedings, what all the different meetings were about and the issues raised in relation to her children's emotional and physical needs. On such occasions, she became confused, anxious, and upset. Her advocate was able to prepare Ruby before meetings, help her understand what was going on and why, and ask for explanations from professionals if things weren't clear.

Other examples of advocate as interpreter:

- accompanying parents to court

- checking benefit entitlements

- explaining the content of official letters

- producing a pictorial shopping list for a mother unable to read or write

- working through a housing transfer form with parents

- helping parents to understand their child's LEA statement

- accompanying parents on visits to the doctor and hospital appointments.

Practice points

- Plain speaking is a virtue when working with parents.

- Double-check that what you say has been understood by parents, especially when you're speaking to them on the phone.

- Never assume that professionals' priorities are parents' priorities when seeking to explain things to parents.

- Accessibility is the touchstone of all communication in advocacy partnerships.

- Be sensitive to how parents see themselves when translating for them. Not all of them accept the labels they are given by agencies or concur with other people's judgements about their competence.

- Parents may be willing to take notice of facts they would otherwise reject when these are communicated by someone they trust.

- Don't allow practitioners to use you as their messenger.

- Don't take anything you're told by the services or by professionals on trust. Always seek written confirmation of promises or agreements.

- Language reveals the person. Make sure you don't lapse into jargon or use words that identify you with professionals or officials.

Difficulties and compromises

- There is a fine line between making information accessible to parents and being seen as a mouthpiece for authority.

- There is a danger of an advocate as interpreter inadvertently undermining a parent's self-esteem.

- Advocates themselves may sometimes be at a loss as to what's going on.

Advocate as listener...

'*She listened to me talk which helped me get through the week.*'

means...

reducing parents' feelings of isolation by enabling them to share their worries, air their grievances or just talk things over.

Sylvia Berryman's support worker called four times a week to help her clean the house, do the shopping and show her how to budget. Sylvia was frequently upset, to the point of tears, by this worker who, she said, humiliated her in public, called her names, constantly criticised her, ordered her about, and allowed her too little control of her own money. She even answered Sylvia's phone when it rang. Her advocate twice witnessed examples of such treatment and saw how it undermined Sylvia's already poor self-image. Although Sylvia was forever voicing her grievances against this worker, she did not want to make an official complaint. She just wanted someone to whom she could off-load.

Irene Sharman and her partner, Tim, had had their only child removed and put up for adoption when she was seven. Irene had never come to terms with the loss of her daughter and still felt a burning anger against those whom she saw as responsible for taking her child away. Irene disliked being left alone in the house when Tim was at work, finding the days long and lonely with nothing to distract her from the hurt inside. She asked her advocate to take her out, and used these trips to vent her feelings about events leading up to the adoption.

Other examples of advocate as listener:

- creating a relationship that allowed parents to feel secure enough to talk spontaneously about sensitive matters such as:
  - stressed marital relations
  - bereavement
  - childhood abuse
  - victimisation and harassment
  - worries about their children
  - complaints and grievances against authority
  - family fall-outs and quarrels
  - anxieties about maintaining contact with children in long-term foster care
  - health worries.

Practice points

- Be prepared to pitch in — helping with the washing up or playing with the children

can be an aid to rapport. You'll often learn more by going shopping with someone than by sitting down to talk.

- Proceed at the parents' pace. They set the frequency of visits and the timetable of work.

- Don't be hurried by the ticking clock. Remember that parents with learning difficulties may need more time to say what they want to say.

- Don't rush parents. You risk making them feel slow and inadequate, and losing their attention. Let them take their time.

- If conversation becomes laboured or seems to be going nowhere, be ready to leave. Don't prolong a meeting for form's sake.

- Beware of excluding partners who are not so ready to talk.

- Taking some age-appropriate books or toys (a supply of paper and colouring pens are always a good stand-by) can help to keep children amused and occupied on visits, and make it easier for parents to talk.

- Questioning can interfere with listening. Learn to wait, watch and be aware.

- Let parents know from the start that they don't have to answer your questions if they don't want to — 'keeping mum' is their privilege.

Difficulties and compromises

- Parents who have accepted their advocate as someone they can talk to may not think twice about contacting them for a chat whenever they are feeling lonely or down or worried, irrespective of the day or time.

- Parents can readily mistake the willingness to listen for a mark of friendship, and advocates can be made to feel guilty (as if they are cheating the parents) knowing they are only doing their job.

- Lonely people, who have rarely had anyone listen to them in the past, can place serious demands on an advocate's time.

- Listening to people's troubles without being able to change their lives can be demoralising for advocates, who are often left feeling ineffectual.

- Some parents found it hard to say they no longer wanted their advocate to call. Advocates had to learn to listen to their silence, and to raise the issue themselves if necessary.

Advocate as scribe...

'She helped me fill in the forms to move house.'

means...

writing letters and helping with form-filling.

Maureen Hobbs suffered from asthma and used an inhaler for relief. Whenever she collected the children from school or did her shopping, she often had to stop a while to catch her breath. Her advocate suggested she applied for Disability Living Allowance. Maureen agreed, and authorised her advocate to obtain a form.

They completed it together, with the advocate reading out the questions and transcribing Maureen's answers. The advocate then wrote one of the supporting statements and Maureen arranged for her GP to submit the other. After the usual checks, Maureen was awarded DLA and £500 in accrued benefits.

Bessie Stove's mother had died two years previously and she still felt her loss keenly. Since the funeral she had lost touch with her stepfather, who lived in a nearby town, and sometimes she felt an overwhelming desire to see him. Her advocate suggested they might send a letter and Bessie, who couldn't read or write, jumped at the idea. It would let him know both her address and telephone number, and that she thought fondly of him. She dictated what she wanted to say and the advocate wrote it down for her to sign.

Other examples of the advocate as scribe:

- writing letters of complaint

- writing to local councillors

- filling in claim forms

- helping to open a bank account

- keeping records of the outcome of meetings with professionals.

Practice points

- Remember to keep parents informed of all communications made with others on their behalf.

- Check with parents every time something is written down. They must always agree what you have recorded.

- Ensure the parents answer the questions when filling in forms. Do not attempt to anticipate their answers, presume what they might say or proceed simply on the basis of your prior knowledge of the family.

- Always write up visits and the outcomes of meetings immediately, or points may be forgotten or remembered wrongly.

Difficulties and compromises

- Beware of allowing the more articulate or able partner to speak for the other. It is only too easy for a silent partner to disappear from the written record, and for their personal needs and interests to be overlooked.

- Care must be taken when writing to, or sharing information with, someone who cannot read, knowing that it will be seen by a third party.

- Be ready to respect the need for confidentiality between partners or family members when the occasion demands.

Advocate as problem-solver...

'Any problems I tell her and she tries to help me.'

means...

taking a holistic view of the family and helping parents to identify the choices they face in dealing with their problems, supporting them in their decisions, and ensuring that practitioners are alerted to options for helping families they may have missed.

Bessie and Gary Stove's social worker told them it was time their five-year-old daughter, Emmy, moved into her own bedroom. Gary knew only too well what was on her mind, but their spare room was full of junk and Gary baulked at the task of clearing it out. Moreover, getting rid of all the accumulated rubbish in the room would call for transport, which they lacked, and decorating it would cost money, when they had none to spare. Their advocate offered to help, and set about motivating them by example. He worked alongside Gary to bag up all the trash and together they carted it to the tip in his car. He arranged for the council to remove some unwanted furniture, and obtained a supply of free paint from a voluntary recycling venture. Gary, Bessie and the advocate all pitched in to decorate the room — blue woodwork with yellow walls. When they'd finished, the advocate got hold of some second-hand furniture through a charity, leaving mum, dad and daughter to arrange the room and hang up Emmy's drawings.

Soon after he moved up into secondary school, Simon Burgess stopped attending and took to staying in bed all morning. His parents tried their best but didn't know how to get him to go. The situation had been going on for some time when their advocate became involved. She contacted the education department, only to be told that he'd been overlooked. A meeting was fixed up between all the parties, at which it was agreed that the education welfare officer would call in the morning and walk Simon to school. This succeeded in getting him on to the premises, but soon after the education welfare officer withdrew, Simon began to revert to his old habits. His parents were deeply worried about him missing his schooling and, after moving to a new house in a different area, they asked their advocate to give priority to getting him into a new school. Extensive negotiations followed with the local authority, whose officials now insisted that Simon should go to a special school, despite the fact that his statement recommended giving support to assist his re-integration in a mainstream placement. The Pupil Referral Service finally agreed to classify him as an 'anxious non-attender' rather than as having 'behavioural difficulties', and to maintain his statement. They frankly acknowledged that this change of heart had come about because of the advocate's involvement with the family. This decision cleared the way for the local secondary school to offer Simon a place. A plan was put in hand to ease his transition back into school following a phased programme of home tuition, outreach support, and part-time attendance.

Other examples of advocate as problem-solver:

- helping families to budget their income

- sorting out ways of dealing with debts

- working with families to resolve difficulties in relationships

- responding to contingencies like a broken cooker or washing machine

- advising parents having difficulties with their children

- mobilising voluntary and community resources.

Practice points

- Don't meddle when things are OK. Don't feel obliged to be doing something. Just keep in touch.

- Work at maintaining trust until you are needed.

- Don't go in to a family and try to fix things right away. Just get to know each other first. There will be plenty of time later for problem-solving.

- When starting with new families, ask what they need help with first and tackle that, even if it doesn't seem to you the most pressing problem.

- Faced with a heap of problems, first tackle the one you can do something about.

- Don't feel you have to fix everything for the family. Just try and help them make things better, and help them feel better about themselves. At least don't make things worse.

- Remain flexible at all times in your dealings with parents. Flexibility is the key to effective advocacy and an antidote to the bureaucracy and red tape of official agencies.

- Be prepared to adjust your way of working to suit the parents, rather than expecting them to fit in with you.

- Be careful how you offer people second-hand clothes, furniture etc. Don't imply you're doing them a favour, and make it possible for them to refuse.

- Always look for a positive way of responding to parents' problems.

- Don't keep doing what doesn't work.

- Parents are often overwhelmed by their problems. Simply naming them can help. Putting them into some sort of order can relieve the pressure and make them seem more manageable.

- Parents should always be presented with clear options and choices and allowed to decide for themselves what course of action they wish to take.

Difficulties and compromises

- Living with the frustration of knowing you can't make people do things but knowing that (sometimes) it might be better if you did.

- Parents often do not grasp the urgency of the situation, appreciate the need for haste, or see the likely knock-on effects of not acting immediately. In such situations there is a strong temptation for the advocate to take over, rather than point out the risks and consequences and then support the parents in whatever decision they make.

- Drawing a line between your role as advocate and that of other practitioners is not easy. You may know what you're about, but it's unlikely the parents will, at least in the beginning.

- Where a family problem originated in the behaviour of one of the partners (for example, money troubles arising from spendthrift habits), it could be very difficult for the advocate to get involved without being seen as taking sides.

- Most parents showed a measure of resourcefulness in coping with their daily lives and many were not averse to using their advocate in much the same way. Advocates had to be clear in their own mind about precisely when supporting

families turned into servicing families, and when to say yes ('Sure, I'll give you a lift to the supermarket on my way back to town') or no ('I'm sorry but I'm not available to pick you up and take you shopping on Wednesday').

- Extended families were a source of both comfort and trouble for parents, sometimes at the same time. Advocates had to tread very softly when dealing with these relationships. Resolving a problem for parents at the expense of alienating family might turn out to be a set-back rather than a solution.

- Advocacy is about working with the grain. This simple maxim can prove difficult in practice, when working with couples whose wishes or interests pull in different directions.

Advocate as fixer...

"We had big holes in the walls and missing doors. She sorted it out."

means...

sorting out problems of service delivery caused by poor co-ordination, errors, oversights and bureaucratic inertia.

Pearl Mitchell's youngest son, Damien, has autism. From the age of fourteen he rarely spoke or left the house. He was finally admitted to hospital, when he was eighteen, for a month's assessment, as a result of which it was agreed that he should be allocated a male support worker whose task would be to get him out of the house, involve him in activities, such as sport, and teach him independent living skills. It wasn't long before Mrs Mitchell began to have doubts about the support worker. He spent long periods talking to her, reading the paper or watching television with Damien, and frequently left early or failed to turn up at all. On their days out, he took Damien to a local shopping mall, leaving him to play the video machines while he met up with a pal. When Mrs Mitchell and her advocate voiced their concerns at a review meeting, the social worker refused to discuss the issue, praising the support worker for the difficult job he was doing, and saying his interest was in Damien's behaviour, not the support worker's. Things continued as before, until the support worker started asking Mrs Mitchell to defray his expenses. At this point, the advocate wrote to the local authority on her behalf requesting clarification of the terms of his contract. It soon became apparent that the support worker had been extracting money from Mrs Mitchell by deception and claiming from his employer for days when he had not shown up for work. Both Mrs Mitchell and Damien felt a sense of relief when he left the scene.

Moira Potter had been referred to a dental surgeon by her community nurse. She hadn't seen a dentist for many years, and some of her teeth had broken off completely, leaving just the roots embedded in the gums. Moira was keen to have them seen to and turned up for

her appointments conscientiously. One day, clearly upset, she told her advocate that she didn't want to go again. It seemed that, on her last visit, the injection hadn't taken and she had been in pain throughout. Moira had left without saying anything, though profoundly disturbed by the experience. Her advocate contacted the dentist to explain the position and enquired about alternative forms of anaesthetic. She was given a choice of two other methods, chose the one she preferred and completed her treatment successfully.

Other examples of the advocate as fixer:

- chasing up service workers who'd missed appointments or who hadn't fulfilled their promises

- dealing with problems thrown up by shortcomings in the services

- helping to secure equipment such as fireguards and safety gates

- searching out sympathetic practitioners.

Practice points

- Remember the 'creaking gate' effect; it is often the small things that grind a parent down. Don't mistake small for minor.

- Don't let the statutory services off the hook by making good their errors and omissions for the sake of the parent.

- Listen to parents for clues that practitioners are adding to their troubles by bad practice.

- Don't feel impelled to do everything yourself. Advocacy is not about delivering a service, but about making sure the services deliver.

- Make alliances with other practitioners and workers to challenge agencies that are not doing what they should be doing.

- Don't allow yourself to be carried away by issues of principle. Take your cue from the parents. It is always their interests that should determine what action you take in cases of bad practice or system failure.

- Part of the role of the advocate is to chivvy practitioners and official agencies into accounting for their actions to the people they affect.

Difficulties and compromises

- Bad practice was a major source of stress for families, yet one of the hardest things for an advocate to tackle. Parents' reliance on the services made redress all the more difficult. Although an advocate had nothing to lose from pursuing a complaint, the parents were often wary of stirring up trouble for themselves.

- Preventing the services from using the presence of an advocate as a pretext for shelving some of their responsibilities.

- Acting as advocate for parents who needed regular support in order to cope but refused to have anything to do with the services following bad experiences in the past.

- Faced with being asked to sort out a problem that appeared to be within the family's sphere of competence, it was not always easy to draw a line between lack of know-how, lack of confidence and lack of effort.

Advocate as conduit...

'She took me to see another mother, Tricia.'

means...

channelling the lessons learnt in supporting one family for the benefit of another.

Ruby Mason and Olive Robinson had the same advocate and both happened to be involved in child-care proceedings at the same time. They also shared the same solicitor. However, the multitude of case conferences, core groups and reviews they had to attend were mostly made up of a cast of different practitioners. Their advocate was able to observe and compare the differences in practice between the teams and feed ideas and examples from one to the other about how to make the process easier for the mothers.

Gillian Tanner and her daughter, Susie, lived with Gillian's mum. Mum paid all the household bills except for the TV licence, which was Gillian's responsibility. When Gillian forgot to renew the licence, they were caught by a detector van. She worked herself into a state, worrying that she'd be sent to prison. Gillian and her advocate approached the licensing authority, which agreed to her paying the arrears and future sums on a monthly basis. When Christine and Graham Humphries found themselves in the same position, the advocate was able to tell them how Gillian had sorted out the problem.

Other examples of the advocate as conduit:

- telling people about voluntary agencies that others had found helpful in the same situation as them

- helping parents handle abusive or nuisance phone calls by explaining how others had dealt with them

- putting parents in touch with each other

- passing on information about grants and other resources from one family to another

- using the knowledge of clued-up practitioners for the benefit of parents whose own support workers lacked such experience or savvy

- drawing on our own growing experience as individual advocates and as a team to improve our ways of working with parents.

Practice points

- Remember that parents may already be receiving possibly conflicting advice and information from different practitioners. Another voice may simply increase the static. It may be wise to clear the lines of communication at the start.

- Parents often react against training. They've either had it up to their necks or they've had bad experiences in the past. Anything that resembles training needs to be presented carefully. Avoid slipping into an 'I-know-best' posture.

- Work to reinforce good advice the parents are receiving from other quarters.

- Create opportunities for bringing parents together.

Difficulties and compromises

- Some fathers made the work of the advocate more difficult by vetoing or subverting help aimed at the mother, which they saw as threatening their own interests. Money was often the bugbear in such instances.

- Empowering a parent in an unequal partnership may seem threatening to the dominant partner.

- Supporting a parent who is dominated by a more able partner or by older children always raised problems of accountability for the advocate.

- No two families are alike, so it can never be assumed that what worked for one will work for another. There is no formula for successful advocacy.

Advocate as sounding-board...

'She was someone to ask things.'

means...

encouraging families to have confidence in their own ability to cope by helping them to work things out for themselves.

Catherine O'Connor and her baby son lived in a tiny flat in a high-rise inner city tenement block. She had recently kicked out her partner on account of his lazy and dirty ways, and his suspect behaviour with their son. She had very little money, and was in poor health, lonely and depressed. Having an advocate helped to bolster her confidence in her ability to manage alone. When her ex-partner started pestering her and making demands about access to their son, she would ring her advocate to talk over what to do and rehearse what she was going to say to him. Knowing there was someone there to listen to her gave her the strength to start building a new life for herself.

Gillian Tanner was beginning to feel she wanted to move out of her mother's house where she lived with her daughter, Susie. She asked her advocate to help her work out the best way to go about getting a place of her own. The situation was complicated, because Gillian's mum had responsibility for Susie, and Gillian was wanting to take her daughter with her. The advocate accompanied Gillian to her solicitor's to check out her legal rights, to an advice centre to find out about her benefit entitlements, and to the area housing office to see if there might be any suitable tenancies available near her mum's. Together they made a list of everything that Gillian would need to furnish a house. Armed with all this information, Gillian used her advocate to rehearse the pros and cons of moving. In the end, she decided to stay where she was for the time being and save her money for when she was ready to set up on her own.

Other examples of the advocate as sounding-board:

- giving time to listen to parents' hopes and ambitions for themselves and their children

- encouraging parents to talk through a decision as a basis for making up their own minds about what to do for the best

- acting as a source of advice when called on by parents who have difficulties managing their own finances

- supporting parents who needed encouragement to branch out and take on new challenges, such as starting an evening class.

Practice points

- Avoid the temptation of offering to help parents with things they have always done for themselves in the past.

- Don't be too ready to offer advice. Saying nothing may sometimes be best.

- At some point, you may have to say 'That's up to you'.

- It is very important to start and end every session with something positive.

- Make a point of praising parents for their own and their children's achievements and progress.

- Parents appreciate having someone to whom they can talk without having to justify themselves, without being made to feel inadequate, and without fearing a telling off.

Difficulties and compromises

- An advocate must steer a narrow course between keeping up parents' morale in the face of the difficulties they are facing and giving them false hopes.

- Boosting parents' confidence was an uphill struggle when all the time other people were putting them down.

- Supporting parents in decisions that you believe would only add to their problems.

Advocate as confidante...

'She kept things confidential, cos its nowt to do with them.'

means...

someone with whom private and confidential information can be safely shared in the sure knowledge that it will not be passed on or used against the family.

Moira Potter's son had been fostered before his first birthday and she now saw him about once a week. She tried to cover the hole in her life by keeping herself busy and searching out company. Most days she attended a drop-in centre, and in the evenings she often went down to watch what was going on in a large sports and leisure centre. Occasionally, though, her loneliness and unhappiness would break through her defences. At such times, if there happened to be willing drinking partners on hand, she would go for a binge to try to blot out the hurt. Afterwards she'd sink into a

depression, and sometimes open a bottle of pills. At some point in this cycle, she'd ring her advocate at home. If Moira was drunk, she could usually be talked out of harming herself and persuaded to go home to bed. On a couple of occasions, though, the first call was from a hospital ward. Moira always wanted her advocate to keep these incidents to herself.

Dilly Alderson lived with her partner, Jim, a wheelchair user, and their three small children. Dilly had confided to her advocate on a number of occasions that she found looking after the different needs of her family emotionally draining. They lived in a cramped, two-bedroom house, with Jim sleeping in the living room. His social worker was sorting out a transfer for them into a property adapted for a wheelchair user. While Dilly cared about Jim, she no longer loved him, and was fearful he would start sleeping with her again if they moved into a bigger house. He also gambled a lot and, Dilly confessed, had recently blown a good part of a community care loan their advocate had helped them secure to buy new carpets. Being able to voice these worries enabled Dilly and her advocate to talk through ways of addressing her needs as an individual in her own right.

Other examples of the advocate as confidante:

- ensuring people felt safe when talking about their experience of physical or sexual abuse

- listening to a parent who wanted to talk about his feelings on finding his father and his wife in bed together

- turning a blind eye to parents who were drawing benefits while doing casual work

- creating a relationship in which people felt free to talk about problems they were having with their children, without fear of the consequences

- working with couples who were at odds with each other where one or both of them wanted to talk privately about their difficulties.

Practice points

- Resist attempts by professionals to see you as one of them.

- Adopt a healthy scepticism about professional assurances of confidentiality. These are too often only honoured in the breach. Confidentiality is widely taken to encompass sharing information with colleagues in the same agency or with others working on the same case.

- Be wary of being used by practitioners as a source of information about parents and families.

- Be prepared to talk about yourself. Advocacy is not a one-way street in which all the information flows from the parent. Giving encourages sharing.

- Meeting outside the home may free people to talk without them having to worry about being overheard by their partner or children.

- Beware of inadvertently divulging confidences when dealing with other members of the family by assuming that they know what you know.

Difficulties and compromises

- Not letting information acquired in confidence from one partner affect your relations as advocate with the other partner or the family.

- Resisting the temptation to disclose information acquired in confidence in order to correct a mistaken judgement or false conclusion reached by a practitioner.

- Being caught between warring partners each seeking to get the advocate on their side, while using the cloak of confidentiality to pursue their grievances against the other.

- Knowing how to respond to people's (generally mothers') often matter-of-fact accounts of their own physical and sexual abuse as children.

Advocate as ally...

'It was good to have someone on my side.'

means...

someone who is unambiguously on the family's side, prepared to stand by them, and whose actions are always consistent with this stance.

The Stoves would have presented concerns to any child protection team. They had two children, aged five and two years, and an older son who'd been adopted. When their advocate began visiting the family, their house was on the verge of chaos. All the signs pointed to a domestic routine that had all but broken down. The floors provided an unhygienic play space for a crawling child, and their young son spent the greater part of his day strapped in his cot or highchair for his own safety. There were moments when their advocate wondered about the well-being of their children. At the same time, she could see that most of their problems were the product of their situation. Trapped in a house they had unwisely bought from redundancy monies and now could not afford to maintain, exploited by neighbours, starved of cash and burdened by debts, they were slowly being ground down by the sapping effects of poverty on their living standards and their motivation. The response of the advocate was to demonstrate by word and action that she had faith in their capacity as a family to overcome their difficulties. As Gary Stove said later, 'I think other families would benefit from having advocates. Families in difficulties like us. It takes a load off our shoulders'.

Olive Robinson's and her partner, Grant's, baby son had already been placed in foster care when they were introduced to their advocate. Allegations about their maltreatment of their son and the cause of his injury were the subject of a long legal action that involved medical investigations, case conferences, reviews, core group meetings, assessments, solicitor's briefings and court appearances. Olive and Grant's advocate accompanied them throughout this ordeal, showing by her presence, as much as what she did or said, that she stood by them, and being available to listen, counsel or sympathise whenever

they wanted someone to talk to whom they could trust. She shared their elation when they won the court case, the anguish of the waiting when social services announced their decision to take the case to the High Court on a technicality, and their despair and grief when the appeal went against them and their son was eventually put up for adoption.

Other examples of the advocate as ally:

- supporting families through complaints and grievance procedures

- standing by families who ran into trouble with neighbours, the police, council officials, or other 'power people'

- challenging examples of 'blaming the victim' where parents were held responsible for things that owed more to shortcomings in the services

- questioning the minutes of official meetings that didn't adequately represent the parents' case

- assisting a family who wanted to change their support worker.

Practice points

- Make sure people know that if they don't wish to see you they only have to say so.

- There's no reason why parents should think you are any different from other people who've let them down in the past, whatever your fine words and assurances. Remember that it's not what you say, it's what you do.

- If you say you're going to do something, don't put it off. Prompt action on promises bolsters trust, gives heart to the parents, and shows you mean business.

- Be punctilious about keeping appointments and arriving on time. Leaving people waiting or not turning up is discourteous and conveys the impression they are not important. Always find some way of letting parents know in advance if an appointment has to be changed.

- If muddles or misunderstandings about appointments should arise, always put them down as your error and apologise.

- When arranging a meeting, first ask parents when would be convenient for them, and then find a mutually convenient date and time. Never require parents to fit in with your diary.

- Never make promises you can't keep.

- Language can be used to put people down, to convey authority, to maintain distance, to imply criticism, to mark status. Pay attention not only to what you say to parents but also to how you say it.

Difficulties and compromises

- An advocate must emphasise parents' positive qualities when all around are focusing on their deficiencies. A person who is uncomfortable with demonstrating this kind of faith in the parents should not be serving as their advocate.

- It is easy for advocates, like parents, to be worn down by repeatedly encountering the same prejudices and discriminatory attitudes among people with the power to mess up families. System abuse undermines advocacy as well as parenting.

- Advocates and parents were frequently inconvenienced by practitioners who failed to consider that they too might have other commitments and who gave short notice of important meetings.

- Advocacy relationships had to be responsive to household changes. They needed to be re-negotiated when partnerships were broken by separation or death, or when a parent took up with a new partner or a grown-up child returned to live at home.

- Where a parent chose to leave a supportive environment and move in with a partner who was known to have a drink problem or to be violent, the advocate could only stand by and be available.

- Supporting a couple was difficult where the advocate felt that one of the partners (almost always a father without learning difficulties) was contributing to the family's problems.

Advocate as sleuth...

'She got us some equipment, a pushchair and some furniture.'

means...

tracking down and searching out information that will help parents achieve positive objectives.

Alice Sykes had been put in a children's home at the age of fifteen after falling victim to a paedophile. While in care she had struck up a relationship with a young man who later turned out to be a Schedule 1 offender, and fell pregnant to him. Her baby was fostered and eventually placed for adoption. Alice was deeply scarred by these two traumas in her young life and confessed to her advocate that she thought she might need help to come to terms with her muddled emotions. Her advocate was able to put her in touch with the Victim Support Scheme and locate a counselling and therapy service that helped women through the loss of a child.

Pearl Mitchell had difficulty finding shoes her size so tended to wear men's trainers. Her doctor advised her to have some shoes made as the trainers were damaging her feet. Her previous experience of surgical shoes was off-putting. She remembered them as clumsy and unfashionable. Her advocate checked out the possibility of having a pair custom-made to order but the price was prohibitive. In the course of her enquiries, however, the advocate discovered that shoes were now provided on the NHS in a wide range of styles, colours and materials, and were free on prescription. Pearl was delighted with her soft, black leather lace-ups with their red trim.

Other examples of the advocate as sleuth:

- making enquiries for a mother wanting an independent assessment

- checking out the availability of Housing Improvement Grants

- finding a course on money management that offered crèche facilities

- locating accessible women's groups, toddler groups, and single parent's groups for a lonely mum

- finding out how best to dispose of an unwanted cat.

Practice points

- Providing parents with information doesn't oblige them to act on it. Leave them to mull it over and decide for themselves in their own time.

- Accompanying people and showing them where to find out for themselves was better than doing it for them.

- Be prepared to experiment with ways of presenting information that make it accessible, like colour-marking dials on the washing machine or drawing up a pictorial shopping list.

- Repetition is an aid to learning and remembering.

- Make a point of including the less able partner even when you think the information may go over their head.

Difficulties and compromises

- Extracting written replies from official agencies to letters.

- Practitioners who consistently fail to return phone calls.

- Practitioners who are unobtainable for days on end.

- Advocates were made to run around in circles and wasted an enormous amount of time following up information from official sources that proved to be unreliable.

Advocate as mentor...

'Things I couldn't cope with I spoke to her about.'

means...

sharing knowledge and experience of life in the capacity of a supportive equal rather than an expert.

Julie Bennett had been prescribed paediatric paracetamol by her GP for her baby's diarrhoea, but she was also giving her Calpol, thinking this would help too. When Julie mentioned what she was giving her poorly daughter to relieve her symptoms, her advocate, having children of her own and knowing that Calpol contained paracetamol, was able to warn her of the danger of exceeding the recommended dose.

A mother talked with her advocate about giving up breast-feeding her baby. She hadn't wanted to broach the matter at the clinic in case her health visitor thought she wasn't coping. She felt they were watching her. The baby always seemed to be hungry, and grizzled a lot. She didn't think he was getting enough milk to satisfy him. Her advocate said she'd had the same problem with one of her children. They discussed the benefits of breast-feeding, and the advocate

encouraged her to do as she'd done and try giving the baby supplementary feeds.

Other examples of the advocate as mentor:

- suggesting to a mother how she might stop her young son from lifting packets of sweets whenever she took him to the supermarket

- discussing with a mother what she might wear for an upcoming court appearance

- helping a family to choose a new living-room carpet

- talking over the risks of keeping a car on the road without MoT or road tax.

Practice points

- Advocacy is more about offering advice than giving advice, and appreciating the difference is what prompts advocates to bite their tongue whenever they hear themselves starting to tell someone what to do.

- Ask and show you value parents' opinions.

- Allow the parents to take the lead. Listen to what they have to say before offering your views.

- Parents have usually had to cope with a lifetime of problems and pressures. Never underestimate their survival skills.

- Don't feel you have to spend all your time talking about people's problems. Helping families lighten up is also part of the advocacy task.

- Don't encourage parents to think that you'll pick up the tab when you're out with them.

- Allow enough time for visits, especially out-of-home excursions, so you don't give the impression of having somewhere more important to go.

- Don't rely on people to remember when next you said you'd call. Write it down for them, so that even if they can't read they can check with someone who can.

- Don't expect parents to keep all their appointments. It's up to them whether they wait in or turn up. Leave a card if you call and the parents are out saying, 'Sorry I missed you'.

- Always defer to the parents if other people show up while you're visiting. Look to them to indicate whether you should stay or go.

- Help parents to think ahead.

Difficulties and compromises

- Having to find ways of by-passing the father to support the mother.

- Getting parents to accept the limits of your own experience and not being drawn into matters beyond your ken.

- Knowing that parents needed the support of the health and social services but fearing that, once professionals became involved, it might lead to consequences the parents would not have wanted for themselves.

- Dealing with situations where parents needed, but were unwilling to seek, expert help of a kind the advocate was not qualified to offer (for example, with health matters, a child's behavioural problems, depression).

Advocate as observer...

'She looks after me.'

means...

keeping a look-out for the early signs of stress or changes in personal circumstances that might impact on the parents' capacity to cope.

After the death of her husband and mainstay, Emily Burgess was given comfort, help and support by her sister and family. A couple of months on, however, they began to wind down their level of involvement. Emily's two older children failed to take up the slack or take on what had previously been their father's responsibilities in the home. Emily struggled with her money, the household chores, and her own care. The house became dirty, there was rarely any food in the pantry nor any sign of them having had a cooked meal. Emily began to look drawn, and her youngest son stopped going to school. The advocate felt the time had come to discuss with the family the option of asking the Community Learning Disability Team to assess Emily's needs.

Christine and Graham Humphries had run up large debts with a catalogue firm and were having their money budgeted by their support worker. They were unhappy about not holding their own benefit books and, when their support worker left, they were keen to prove that they could manage their own affairs. Christine and Graham asked their advocate if she would keep a weather eye on their spending. When Graham registered for cable TV, she pointed out that they might have problems maintaining the monthly payments. The advocate soon saw that Christine was indeed finding it harder to eke out her housekeeping, and reminded them that their TV licence was overdue for renewal. Three months later they pulled out of their contract.

Other examples of the advocate as observer:

- An advocate needed to be alert to an array of indicators that might signal potential trouble ahead, including:
  - an unexpected pregnancy
  - the arrival of a lot of bills close together
  - frequent illnesses and feeling run down
  - arguments with extended family who gave support
  - marital troubles
  - broken appliances such as a cooker or washing machine
  - a supportive practitioner moving on
  - a parent acting out of character
  - children frequently missing school.

Practice points

- Don't lose contact just because things are going smoothly. Show you welcome parents getting in touch with you just for a chat.

- There is no substitute for knowing the parents really well.

- Routine is the enemy of effective advocacy. Be ready to re-appraise your role in response to changes in the family's situation or the make-up of the household.

- Be aware of how parents' competence can be undermined by people who try to run their lives for them.

- Always look beyond people's learning difficulties when searching for the cause of their troubles.

- Keep an eye on the effects of changes in the parents' family and social circle — the arrival of a new support worker, an older child leaving home, close relatives moving away, the birth of another baby — for any signs that they are not managing as well as before.

Difficulties and compromises

- Watching parents who had had their children taken away turn on each other.

- Trying to anticipate problems and forestall difficulties was so often frustrated by the short-term, crisis-driven nature of the statutory services, which generally only stepped in after an emergency had occurred (and then proceeded to blame the parents for its happening).

- Working with the inequities built into the service system. These inequities meant, for example, that access to resources depended more on your address than your needs, and ensured that some families survived where similar families elsewhere went under. One single mother, whose only child was in long-term foster care, was receiving support from a community nurse, a disability social worker, and three volunteers who took turns to keep her company in the evening. Two other single mothers, each looking after three young children, were receiving only monthly visits from a health visitor even though both had asked for help from the social services.

Advocate as mover and shaker...

'She helped me get DLA.'

means...

making things happen.

Two mothers who'd met through their mutual advocate independently expressed a wish to meet up some time on their own, though needed a helping hand to bring them together. After one of them had been through a gruelling court case about the residency of her child, the advocate took the other round to her house so they could talk about what had happened. 'I see a good person in her', said the visiting mum of her friend, 'and going to see her, I hope, does her some good and it might do me some good too.'

With three small children and a fourth on the way, Sam Rhodes felt overwhelmed by his responsibilities and that he had

no life of his own. He shared his feelings with his advocate, saying he thought he might cope better at home if he had an outside interest and the company of some other adults now and again. They talked over the sort of activities that he might like to try and Sam settled on an evening woodwork class, though he'd never done anything like it before and was nervous at the prospect. He decided he'd like to make a coffee table. His advocate cleared the way for his enrolment, persuading the Special Needs Tutor that he should be allowed to attend a regular class without having to jump the hurdle of going through an assessment to prove his ability beforehand. They priced up the materials and bought them together, and then his advocate went along with Sam to show him the ropes and give him some personal support in class. Sam finished his table. Next year, he declared, he'd do it again — on his own.

Other examples of the advocate as mover and shaker:

- saving a family's holiday by transporting them to and from the seaside caravan they had booked

- bringing people together to form a support group

- getting a family out of unfit accommodation

- calling in the morning and accompanying a child to school

- putting a mother in touch with her estranged sister

- persuading relatives of the need to rally round and support a family in crisis.

Practice points

- Being a catalyst isn't the same as being in control. The advocate has to step aside as soon as possible.

- Parents should not be expected to put up with a worse service from statutory agencies than you'd expect for yourself.

- Resist the temptation to push parents into acting quicker than they are inclined.

- Help parents to keep appointments by accompanying them if necessary.

- Don't underestimate the importance of practical help. Helping parents to put their house in order or catch up on neglected home maintenance can make their home a more pleasant place in which to live and make maintaining it more worthwhile.

- Always keep in mind the fact that parents find it difficult to say no to people (you included).

- Make explicit the limits of what you can do and be prepared to explain them more than once.

Difficulties and compromises

- Sometimes parents expected too much of their advocate and became disillusioned as a result.

- Like the parents before them, advocates too encountered feelings of exhaustion and resignation in the face of a seemingly never-ending battle with the service system.

- Parents' reluctance to seek or accept support from professionals and official agencies put a brake on the advocate's ability to mobilise support.

Chapter Eight

Perspectives on Advocacy

What the parents said about their advocate

All but one of the families in at the end of the project who had received one-to-one advocacy support agreed to talk to someone other than their advocate about what it had meant to them. This is what they said.

Pearl Mitchell

Pearl is very independent. She has three grown-up children. Her youngest son has autism. All three lived with her at the beginning of the project. She had been dissatisfied for a long time with her social worker and the support worker who came to help her with her son.

> 'She [Pearl's advocate] sorted out the social work things, writing letters, telephoning people for me, as she could put it in a different way than I could. She visited me when I needed her. She helped me to ask questions at meetings by using her notes in my file. Either she asked the questions, or I did with her help if I couldn't remember. She would visit and help me with meetings when they were held in my house. I was very happy with the way she helped me. I don't think she could do much more. She was someone to talk to. If you like someone, you can open up to them and I could with her. She was all right. Better than that stupid social worker. I hated him. She was someone to ask things and she would help

> you if she could. She is a lot better than a social worker.'

Maureen Hobbs

Maureen was recently divorced from her husband. She has five children. Her two daughters and youngest son, Liam, live with her, and the two older boys live with her ex-husband.

> 'She [her advocate] helped me get DLA and dealt with all the legal side of it. She helped me fill in the forms for moving house and met me at the hospital when Liam had appointments. She helped with him. She was great with me. She helped me more than a social worker and was more useful than a social worker. It was good to talk to someone. I'm still waiting for a house and I would have liked her to have been here to help with that. She helped me more than anyone. We got on great with her and had some laughs. She was some-one to talk to. She was company during the day. It was good to have help; it was good what she did. I would have liked her to have continued coming to see me and helping me. I wish she was still coming.'

Moira Potter

Moira has one child, a son, aged seven. He had been removed from her care before his first birthday and now lives with Moira's sister. Moira sees him about once a week.

'She [her advocate] got me a community nurse. I can ring her up to talk. She got me more involved with Stewart [her son]. She spoke to the dentist for me. I think she did everything she could. It would have been good if she was around when going to court about Stewart. She was all right, helping you to do things, treated me the same all the time. She is a friend.'

Olive Robinson and Grant

Olive and Grant had their first child, a son, removed on suspicion of non-accidental injury. After a protracted legal battle, during which Olive became pregnant again, the child was eventually adopted.

Olive:

'She [her advocate] tells me to calm down when I get stressed up. I lose my temper every time with the social worker. I found it easier at solicitor's cos she used to explain things. Some days she couldn't come cos she had to see other families. She looks after me. She said yesterday at meeting, "Can you get a cushion for Olive?" I had a lot of backache.

She sometimes does minutes at SSD meetings. She's writing every little thing down, and the social worker don't like it. She never forgets. It's more than what they've done and better. My social worker once said to her, "You're not writing this down, are you?", and she said, "I bloody am". She said, "I don't miss a thing". She passes them to me but Grant reads them first. We think they're ever so good. She kept things confidential cos it's nowt to do with them. They keep things from us so why shouldn't we keep things from them?

She's done more than what anyone else has done. I just wish she was still with us. I would have liked her to have continued. I wish she'd have bloody kept on.'

Grant:

'She's always been there. She's been a diamond. She keeps me under control. Been there as a mate. She believed all I said and hasn't doubted me for a minute. I know I haven't done anything but only a few have believed me.'

Bessie and Gary Stove

Bessie and Gary have three children, although their eldest son was adopted when he was three years old. Gary is responsible for most of the domestic jobs and for making sure their daughter Kate attends school a mile away. The family had two advocates to address the different needs of the mother and father, and the different pressures bearing on the household.

Gary:

'John [Advocate 1] has helped by doing all odd jobs such as painting, concreting and repairing the roof. He has saved us money or we would have had to get contractors in. He helped a great deal. I don't think Jane [Advocate 2] could do what he did but she did help but not in the same way. I would like John to continue for ever. He was vital. He helped with jobs we couldn't afford to do, helped me a lot. We would be happy for Jane to come. She helped Bessie more than me and she helped with bills and information. John helped with all jobs, things that needed doing. Jane sorted out our enquiries. We thought they were both OK. We would like them to come and do the same things again. We need outside

help. I have a lot on my plate and need help to do things as I am always busy with the kids. I think other families would benefit from having advocates. Families in difficulties like us. It takes a load off our shoulders.'

Bessie:

'Jane helped by running Gary to school sometimes to pick up Kate. She got us some equipment, a pushchair and some furniture. She helped me write to my dad. I would have liked John to take us into town so I could get a fur-lined jacket. He saved us money when we went on holiday. He took us and picked us up which saved us taxi fares. We had a meal on the way down.'

Elizabeth Rhodes

Elizabeth and her husband, Sam, have four children who live with them (one was born during the project). They have a large number of practitioners calling on them almost daily. The family was provided with two advocates to meet the different needs of both parents, both of whom have learning difficulties. The problem, Elizabeth said, was that it added to the pressure on their time: 'We weren't getting out so much because of all people coming to house.'

'Anne [Advocate 1] *has been right good. Talking and playing with kids. She helped with our daughter's school — but she's still not allowed to go to nearest school. We had big holes in walls and missing doors. John* [Advocate 2] *and community nurse sorted it out. John did all the decorating upstairs. My Sam doesn't like heights. I would like Anne to continue, and kids would. John has become a friend. He says he's going to keep coming.'*

Ruby Mason

Ruby lives with two partners, one of whom, Stan, is the father of her four children who are in foster care. Her fifth child has been adopted. By the time the project had finished, Ruby was still awaiting the date for a final court hearing to decide on the residency of her children.

'I've been heartbroken in front of her [the advocate]. *I'm taking overdoses. She explains to me what I don't understand, what social services are talking about. If I didn't understand what questions were, she'd repeat it and explain it. She was brilliant. Helped me with debts. Had problems with money — still have problems. Calming me down when I get stressed. Any problems I tell her and she tries to help me. Trying to help us get kids back. She went to court with me and review meetings. That's why I want her back. Social worker's a cow.*

I have arthritis and depression. If I'm in bad distress I tell her and she tells me who to get in touch with. I've never had anyone better, not like her before. There's only my solicitor now.'

Stan, the children's father, added, *'All I can say is that she was brilliant for Ruby'.*

Tricia Fraser

Tricia's daughter, Stephanie, had been placed in the care of Tricia's own mother and step-father. Tricia was unhappy about this arrangement. After the final court hearing, which Tricia lost, she went back to live with her husband from whom she had been separated.

'I can't remember what she [her advocate] *actually did, as I have problems with my*

memory. I was happy with her. I would have liked her to have got Stephanie back for me, but I know she couldn't do that. I'd have liked her to continue to help me fight to get Stephanie back. It was good to have someone on my side. I wouldn't want her every week, but just to be there to talk to and if I needed help with anything. She was a friend and supported me when I needed help or advice. But I'm not keen on the word "advocate".

I think she did help me. It was good to be able to talk about problems and to have someone, not in my family, to believe in me, someone from the outside who was more helpful.'

Patricia Ward

Patricia has two children, a boy and a girl. Her daughter, the elder, was adopted a few years ago. She is bringing up her son, Michael, on her own. She had a few boyfriends during the course of the project before settling down with Rob.

'She [her advocate] helped me fill in the forms to move house and we went to housing. She got me interested in going to a group with Michael. I was very happy with the way she helped me. She was someone to talk to and she was great with Michael. I'd rather have her than a social worker. She was good. I could have a laugh with her, she didn't criticise me. She respected things we told her. I liked the confidentiality if we said anything about social workers. I think single parents would benefit from having someone like her. She was great.'

Dilly Alderson and Jim

Dilly and Jim live with their three small

children. Jim uses a wheelchair and has a disability social worker. Dilly has no support for herself. At the start of the project they lived in a two-bedroom house and Jim slept in the living room. They moved into a larger, more accessible house just before the project ended.

Jim:

'I didn't have much to do with her [the advocate]. We had a set-to one week but that was because I was in a lot of pain. It was more to do with me and Dilly rather than her, who I blamed. She was very nice with kids, very kind. She bought them a video at Christmas. I'd give her 10 out of 10. With her coming, we used to discuss our problems more. Before we used to shout at each other. If something was bothering Dilly, she'd bottle it up. Now she's more open and we can talk about things and do something about it.

If Dilly mentioned something to her she'd try and sort it out. If she said she was going to do something, she'd do it. She always asked first. She didn't impose herself. She gave Dilly that bit of a push to go to the resource centre.'

Dilly:

'When I met her I was feeling bad about myself and I wasn't getting out. She helped me go on a course at the resource centre. I didn't know how to cope with three kids and Jim, being disabled. And because of the house we all got on to each other. Sometimes I told her my feelings.

She was a bit too soft sometimes. She used to panic a bit, like when we went to the park with the other families she kept counting the children. She spoke well in what she was saying. I don't think she was a 'care' person, like a social worker. Heart were there but she got too involved in me and the family. She couldn't take things about herself, like a joke. We were on about pop and she said "squash" and we were all having a laugh, but she didn't like it. She got too involved in certain things. If Jim was here, he'd agree with me about her personal side.

I was going to give her a little present for everything what she's done, like a bunch of flowers or a card. I might do anyway. I liked her as a person. She was good to talk to.'

Catherine O'Connor

Catherine lives in a small, one-bedroom, high-rise flat with her young son. She has recently split up with her partner, the baby's father. Contact arrangements between father and son are still being negotiated.

'She [her advocate] told me about the legal and court side of my case, the boring and long-winded process. She has been supportive and talked to my dad, explaining things to him. She took me to see another group member, Tricia. She listened to me talk which helped me get through the week. She was useful for all the information. She is a friend and it was good that she and the group have been there.

I'd like her to be able to come to court with me in October so she could help me with the court process but I know she can't.'

Emily Burgess

At the start of the project, Emily lived with her husband, Eric, and her two sons, Jack and Simon, on a large estate where they suffered constant victimisation. Shortly after they moved house, Eric killed himself.

'She [her advocate] got me a community nurse, helped us to move and helped us by looking at the house before we moved to see if it was OK. She came to the inquest and helped when Eric died. She helped Simon by taking him to school and by getting him a home teacher. She talked to housing and got us the money. She's been a friend to me. She has helped and is someone to talk to. I would have liked to have her around a bit more. I wasn't always able to talk to her on the phone. She was a good friend.'

Stella Bailey

Stella lives with her two young sons, Bobby and Stephen, and a partner who comes and goes. She is expecting her third child.

'She [her advocate] visited me at home in the beginning. When she came she used to play with Bobby. Bobby used to listen to her when she spoke to him. If she'd tried to talk to me without playing with Bobby, she wouldn't stand a chance. Things that I couldn't cope with, I spoke to her about, children mostly. Bobby being naughty and stealing from shops. She told me ways to stop him. Like I didn't know where the Children's Hospital was and she met me outside and came with me to children's hearing test. It helped having her there. She could look after Stephen while Bobby had his test. I was very, very happy with her. I gave her a photo of Bobby and Stephen.'

Summary of parents' views

- All parents were happy with their advocate.

- All parents would have liked their advocate to have continued beyond the end of the project.

- Parents liked receiving copies of what had been written about them ('No-one writing things you didn't know about') and what the advocate was doing for them ('It reminded me of what she'd done and how far things had been done. It reminded her as well.').

- The roles played by the advocates were valued by the parents.

- The only criticisms voiced by parents were about advocates' level of involvement.

What the practitioners said about advocacy

Practitioners were invited to give their views on what impact, if any, the advocates' work had had on their clients, their own practice and on their agency. Comments were obtained by postal questionnaire from eight people who had been closely involved with parents in a professional capacity throughout the project. Some families in the project had no close involvement with a practitioner and there was no-one to ask. In seven cases the practitioner failed to return the questionnaire. This is what those who replied wrote:

Pearl Mitchell's social worker's team manager

'My client having an advocate felt like a very positive move which could help in the understanding of the client's needs amid other complex family needs. The advocate listened to our client and made requests on her behalf to SSD. Some of these requests challenged the systems in place as well as some working practices. Our client clearly felt able to express her concerns about

services to the advocate. On occasions the advocate's emphasis on the client's needs masked some of the wider needs of the family. In a complex case there are many views and needs to be met. The advocate was challenging and this can be very positive in helping us examine our practice. Our client has appeared more assertive, making her own requests. Sometimes these have been unrealistic. However it is positive that they are made.'

Maureen Hobbs' health visitor

'I felt that an advocate was necessary, and felt unable to fill the role myself because of the other demands of my caseload. The client has been getting a level of support that our agency is not always providing. I spend less time contacting other agencies, such as Housing Benefits advice. She had an advocate she was able to contact when needed. She also had time set aside for herself. The client appeared to have confidence in the advocate and some improvement in her level of self-esteem.

From my point of view, there was more time for other priorities within the case load. [The problem is] *that when the advocate's work is completed there is no replacement and she will probably get less support. Is it the health visitor's role to give the time and help needed with this type of client, or should other agencies be involved? The health visitor is there to discuss health and health needs. SSD and FSU were contacted but had no worker available. I would like to see a project like this one continuing. Health visitors would be in a position to make many appropriate referrals.'*

Moira Potter's community nurse

'My client has difficulties in asserting herself, and having someone to talk to about difficulties who would advise and support her really helped her in life. [It helped me too] in having another person to consult when problems occurred, and it was good to know that there were other people that she could turn to. My client has benefited greatly from being with a group of people in a similar situation to herself. She gained confidence in meeting and talking to other people. I aim to continue developing this with her. She was also consulted regularly and asked to participate in sessions which promoted the work of that group.

The advocate dealt with areas which I would have found difficult, having not had the necessary experience, and allowed me to concentrate on other areas of need in the client's life. I felt that my client was getting help from the most relevant people. [The advocate's presence also] made me try to make sure that I carried out work promptly before I was reminded that something had not been done.

My client is sorry that the project has ended — although she has other places to go she feels that the group gave her support and insight that she may find difficult to get elsewhere. It's a shame that funding was not available for the work to continue.'

Olive Robinson's solicitor

'[My client having an advocate] was helpful to me when at court/meetings as I could be more certain she understood events. It also helped the client's confidence. She was very supportive. The advocate was able to provide additional information which I could utilise for the benefit of the client.

It's a service which is beneficial and should continue.'

Olive Robinson's psychologist

'I felt generally positive about my client having an advocate, though some concerns. At first, I felt there was a very anti-professional stance and assumptions being made. This dissipated over time. An advocate generally helps to represent the client view — the user perspective — but it's hard to give specifics. She gave support and empowerment in context of legal/care proceedings. She helped client express anxiety/give feedback about my assessment. Client and sometimes professionals depended on support of advocate — because they found it helpful/valued it. The advocate's involvement proved positive when there, negative when it stopped.

I have found contact with the project and its workers positive — hope it is groundwork on which to build more partnership to pursue support and empowerment of parents with learning difficulties.'

Bessie and Gary Stove's social worker

'Excellent facility which needs to be ongoing. It complemented our service — we try to work in a non-oppressive, enabling way — and added aspects to the service offered by us. The advocate's work was supportive and practical help given. The clients found the work done invaluable. They have begun to do some things for themselves. I would see the need for a permanent advocacy service to be offered to all clients with learning disabilities.'

Elizabeth and Sam Rhodes' community nurse

'Initially, my clients having an advocate took some getting used to, feeling as if my work was being scrutinised. However I actually found this useful, enabling me to reflect on practice. Throughout, I felt this to be beneficial to the clients concerned. [The advocate] assisted them in negotiations with other agencies and ours. Raised self-esteem and confidence. They had a 'positive' friend — a good role model. Helped in lots of practical ways — which I personally feel is what parents want from all of us.

It helped me enormously, too. Giving clients support in areas that often I had little time to give to enabled me to work more effectively in relevant areas, therefore meeting needs across a wider spectrum for the client. We shared tasks, debated issues, shared information, covered each other's absences in terms of contact points. We met regularly and evaluated our input and client progress. Professional isolation was reduced.

Problems arose when an additional advocate became involved — simply because of numbers of people helping and visiting. I feel there is a fine line between promoting independence and confidence and inadvertently creating dependence.

I felt they gained in confidence and learned a lot via role modelling. I felt they learned to have expectations of services, where previously they appeared to accept whatever was offered — appropriate or not. There needs to be long-term commitment to projects like this. People were just gaining confidence, trusting and tentatively making friends when everything stops. Clients' comment — "nothing changes".'

Ruby Mason's social worker

'I felt very pleased that they would be represented. It was beneficial that they had someone to represent their views. Also someone that they perceived as being "on their side". It was extremely beneficial too in terms of "protection" for the social workers. I am unsure if it did have an impact on the agency.

Throughout this case, myself and my colleague were constantly examining our practice. The presence of an advocate did not alter this. It was felt that the advocate sometimes put words into the client's mouth, i.e. interpreting their views in a way that the client had not originally intended. I have seen no change in these clients that could be attributed to the advocate's presence.'

Summary of practitioners' views

- All the practitioners felt their clients had benefited from having an advocate.

- All the practitioners cited ways they had benefited from the work of the advocate(s), though some also found aspects of the advocates' work unhelpful.

- All but one said the advocacy relationship had a positive impact on them or their agency.

- Only two practitioners did not report any positive changes in their client as a result of the advocate's involvement.

- Most practitioners said working alongside an advocate had prompted them to examine their own practice.

- Nearly all the practitioners said they would like to see a permanent advocacy scheme established.

Chapter Nine
The Support Groups

talking together — learning together — helping together — laughing together —
weeping together — being together — parents together

This chapter describes how the support groups were set up, what they did and what the parents gained from attending them. It also looks at some of the wider lessons that came out of the experience of running the groups.

Setting up and getting started

The first task was to find suitable premises. This proved more difficult than we had anticipated. We had drawn up a list of practical requirements, determined partly by project considerations but mostly by the needs of parents. A worker and two of the parents checked out possible venues. They looked for accommodation that provided:

- a large, comfortable, private room

- a kitchen, toilet and store for equipment

- either a playspace for children (with toys) or a crèche close by

and that was:

- easily accessible by public transport or near to parents' homes

- in a safe location

- not connected with health or social services

- affordable

- preferably in a building or setting that catered for a mix of people

- smart enough to bolster parents' sense of self-worth.

Two workers generally attended every meeting. (Having two was necessary to help the parents look after any young children and to ensure continuity during holidays and sickness.) It was agreed from the start that they would adhere to an advocacy role in supporting the self-help aims of the groups, following the principles and guidelines outlined earlier in this report. Particular importance was attached to three points:

- The role of the advocate as facilitator was to assist and support the groups, but not to lead or take responsibility for the meetings. This did not mean standing on the edge of the group. It meant joining in and sharing without taking over.

- The parents owned the groups. After the first meeting, they decided who could join. No-one was invited without their consent.

- The agenda for the meetings should be decided (or left undecided) by the parents.

The only decision taken by workers at the start without reference to parents was that everyone should make their own way to group meetings. This decision was taken for practical and principled reasons. On a practical level, the project did not have the resources to transport everyone, and providing some people and not others with lifts might have proved divisive. On grounds of principle, we were aware from previous experience of the danger of transporting people to places when they didn't want to go. Finding their own way to meetings was a way of ensuring that parents' attendance remained voluntary.

Most new parents were met off the nearest bus or somewhere nearby and shown how to get to the meeting room the first time they attended the group. This also served to ease their introduction to the other parents. Some parents had to be met more than once before they felt confident enough to come on their own.

None of the parents had attended a support group before, nor any other sort of group in which they were in charge. During the course of the first few meetings, they decided on some basic ground rules about how the groups would operate.

- They agreed when to meet, how often and for how long.

- People could come and go whenever they wanted.

- What people said was private and must not be told to outsiders.

- Children under school age could attend with their parents.

- The groups were open to all parents (no mention was made in this context about the groups being for parents with learning difficulties).

- Everyone present should help set up the meeting and tidy up afterwards.

- A different person would lead the meeting each week.

Who came to the groups

City Group met sixty-one times (for two and a half hours each session) in a town-centre venue over a period of eighteen months. During this time, nine mothers, three fathers and three children attended meetings, of whom five mothers and one child turned up almost every week.

District Group met eighteen times (for one and a half hours each session) in a local branch library, with adjacent crèche facilities, over a period of five months. During this time, four mothers with ten children attended meetings, of whom all but one mother and two children came regularly.

Not all the parents who participated in the project attended a support group. There were 25 families involved in the **Parents Together** project. Parents from 13 of these families came to group meetings at some time. Others did not attend for a variety of reasons:

- because the meetings clashed with other commitments

- because they would have needed help with using buses

- because they were frightened of travelling alone

- because they lacked the confidence to attend

- because they were not interested.

What the groups did

Process

The parents were adamant from the beginning (contrary to the expectations and intentions of the workers) that they did not want outside speakers or any experts coming along to talk or join in group meetings. Their position was that if they wanted to know something 'we'd do better to find out for ourselves and bring it back to the group'. Also the idea of sitting and listening did not appeal. They much preferred to do the talking themselves.

The workers kept a record of what was said, what happened and what was decided at meetings, with the parents' permission. Initially, this was done for research purposes (as part of the monitoring of the action project), but as time went on it became an integral part of the workings of the group.

- People liked seeing what they had said being written down. They would often check that the worker had noted it all or say 'Have you got that down?'. People seemed to gain confidence from feeling they had made a contribution.

- Late-comers could be brought up to date with what had gone on in the meeting, using the parents' own language.

- It was useful as a reminder of where we had got to in the previous meeting and what we had left over to do at the next.

- It was a way of continually re-affirming the parents' ownership of the group by demonstrating that the proceedings were driven by what they said.

- It served as a tangible sign that there was no hidden agenda concerning the business of the group.

Keeping the groups together and going meant keeping everybody involved and interested. Attention had to be given to group maintenance as much as to task performance. This was especially important whenever new parents joined a group. Relationships had to change to include them. The first response of established members was often one of apparent indifference or suspicion (even though they had agreed to the new person joining), and the workers had to be ready to break the ice. Members were asked to explain about the group to newcomers.

One successful method of introducing new people into the group was to invite everyone, including workers, to bring along family photos or holiday snaps to show. They allowed for questioning without it seeming nosy or intrusive, enabled people to talk about themselves and each other, and provided a starting point for learning about who we were.

The groups had to handle some strong emotions. Painful feelings (anger, frustration, jealousy, and grief among others) were generated within the groups and brought into the groups. These had to be dealt with in different ways. The initial response to problems in relationships between members was to leave them to sort things out among themselves. Observing and learning how to resolve such conflicts in a safe setting was a positive aspect of the work of the groups and contributed to greater self-awareness and assertiveness among members. If, however, these conflicts continued to the point where they upset others or threatened to split the group, the worker would have to step in to calm matters — always without taking sides. Painful feelings brought into the group were almost always caused by problems in family relationships or by system abuse. These feelings worked to bring the group together, mainly because others had invariably experienced them too. Sharing them with the group created opportunities for showing mutual support, and helped to free people from the sense of being alone in a hostile world.

Activities

Group sessions were not pre-planned or designed with any purpose in mind other than to bring the parents together. From the outset, the aim was that the groups should be a resource for their members, and the parents would decide how they wanted to use them. Topics and tasks were carried over from one week to the next and, as the range of activities the groups were involved in grew, so the agenda of upcoming meetings filled with things to do and decisions to make. Nevertheless, there is no sense in which the groups could be said to have followed a structured programme beyond the routine that emerged as they went along. Looking back, however, it is possible to see that group activities clustered under a number of headings.

The weekly newsround

At the start of each session, everyone, including the workers, talked in turn about things that had happened to them during the past week or since their last meeting, or raised some matter that was troubling them or had made them feel good or which they thought the group would be interested in hearing about. The newsround was very popular. Initially used as an 'ice-breaker' when the groups first formed and people didn't know each other, it soon became a fixture on the weekly agenda. Everyone made a point of always contributing. Some people wrote down their news so they didn't forget anything, and two even bought diaries for the purpose. Others got involved in things they might not otherwise have done in order to

ensure they had something to report. The newsround served a number of purposes:

- It ensured everyone who attended meetings had their own slot on the agenda, a chance to speak, and to have people listen to them.

- It allowed people to get to know each other better, and to appreciate what they had in common.

- It gave everyone a stake in the group.

- It helped to identify issues of common concern.

- It provided an anchor for meetings and gave them a sense of cosy familiarity.

Discussion slots

Discussions usually took place spontaneously in response to parents' news, or questions, worries and concerns that emerged during the course of the meetings. A list of topics raised by parents and discussed within the groups over the course of the project is shown below:

- abuse
- being pushed around
- benefits
- birthdays/treats and special occasions
- child removal
- children
- confidentiality within the group
- conflicts with neighbours
- contraception/pregnancy and birth
- cooking
- death and bereavement
- disability
- education and enrolling at college
- family and home
- fines/debts/money/finances
- harassment/victimisation/burglary/crime
- health – personal and children's

- holidays and trips
- house decorating
- housing matters
- informal support
- jobs and job opportunities
- leisure interests
- loneliness
- making new friends
- male friends
- men who abuse
- moving house/setting up home
- new clothes
- New Year's resolutions
- people from other countries
- pets/animals and plants
- relationships
- religion
- safety and self-protection
- service provision and shortfalls
- travel and mobility
- unemployment.

This list is instructive because it reflects the parents' priorities and their sense of who they are:

- It is not just about being a parent or bringing up children.

- It does not encompass the kinds of concern that usually feature in training programmes for parents with learning difficulties, which are usually child-focused and skill-based.

- It shows that the problems that figure prominently in their lives, and the things that interest them as parents, are probably the same as those of most families in need and do not stem from their learning difficulties alone.

- The focus is on their place in the world, not on their limitations. What they looked for was help with the things that made their lives more difficult.

Occasionally parents volunteered to talk about some subject they knew about (for example, electrical safety, using British Sign Language, cooking). They often brought in letters for advice on how to respond. They made a point of picking up information leaflets likely to be useful to other parents (such as maps of the general hospital, money-saving offers, information on services) and bringing them to the group. Over time, too, individuals became known for having expertise in certain areas, for example, the local bus and tram network. All this served:

- to demonstrate that the group was made up of people with abilities

- to allow people's strengths to come to the fore

- to enable people to learn from others

- to allow people to feel pro-active.

Outings

The groups organised five outings and held a joint meeting with a parents' group from another town. The outings were planned, organised and paid for by the parents:

- a day trip to the Heights of Abraham
- lunch and ten-pin bowling
- picnic in a park
- meal at McDonald's
- meal at a restaurant.

Arranging the outings took up a lot of time in the groups, spread over many weeks. They involved the parents in setting up a bank account, running a savings scheme, finding information about where to go, working out costs, sorting out transport, managing the children — and resolving all the differences that arose within the group about most of these issues! The outings were important because:

- The parents and workers enjoyed them.

- They were something to look forward to and to think about afterwards. As one parent said, 'We want some sweets in our life, not all sours.'

- The fun was in the sharing. 'It was nice to go, even just going to McDonald's for a meal with others instead of sitting there alone with three kids. Kids could meet others too.'

- They provided a lighter side to the groups.

Projects

Parents worked together on a number of projects on their own initiative arising from their ideas:

- They designed an invitation card for prospective members of the group.

- They produced a pictorial leaflet explaining what the group was about to accompany the invitation card, and also for distribution to practitioners and other outlets.

- They put together a small booklet advising families what to look for when moving house. This came about when a family in City Group was anxious about making a move, and asked the group for advice on what to do for the best. Members decided their pooled experience would be useful to other people needing guidance.

- They worked on a healthy-eating pictorial shopping list for people who couldn't read. Over a number of weeks, parents collected recipes and information, discussed a healthy diet and tested out ideas for a leaflet within the group.

Many of the benefits derived from these activities mirrored those listed above under **Discussion slots**. In addition, these projects:

- made members feel the group was important in its own right, as a way of helping other families

- gave people the feeling that they had something to contribute

- allowed them to feel they could get things done.

Student training sessions

Parents Together was asked to present three sessions for student practitioners. Support group parents agreed to accept these invitations, and none chose not to take part.

Session 1: Six mothers and two fathers supported by three project workers led a ninety-minute workshop for a class of DipSW students.

Session 2: Five mothers supported by three project workers presented a ninety-minute workshop for five student community nurses and their tutor.

Session 3: Seven mothers supported by three project workers led a ninety-minute workshop for eight student community nurses.

The preparation for these sessions was lengthy and time-consuming, taking up the best part of four support group meetings. It involved working out with parents what they wanted to say and what they didn't want to talk about, rehearsing the presentation, practising speaking in front of a group, making arrangements for getting to the session, sorting out child-care if required and calming people's nerves and giving them confidence.

The parents found taking part in the sessions very stressful, but each time were ready to repeat the exercise and said they would like to do more. They had never done anything like it before. They had been the focus of attention in many formal meetings, but always as the person being talked about, never the one doing the talking.

> 'It gave us the opportunity to talk about ourselves and hopefully it will help them improve their services to us.'

> 'I was a bit scared at first. All staring at you. It was like Mastermind. But I enjoyed it. I'd do it again.'

> 'It wasn't something I'd have done a couple of years ago. I haven't been to a discussion group before. Before I'd have just sat there and not said anything.'

> 'The student sessions were good. But I think we threw the students in at the deep end.'

> 'I was wary at first. It took a bit of getting used to. I felt a bit uncomfortable the first student session I did. I found it difficult to talk about things.'

> 'I enjoyed the students. I think they'll be better for talking to us.'

Parents were empowered by their experience of these sessions in all sorts of ways:

- It made them feel important.

- They felt they were doing something to right the wrongs done to them.

- People were seen to be listening to them.

- They were free to speak their minds without fear of the consequences.

- It gave them a chance to tell their story.

- They derived strength from the backing of the group.

Difficulties and compromises

The groups were not all plain sailing for either advocates or parents.

Membership

- With the parents owning the groups, it was not the workers' responsibility to control whom they brought along. The practical effect was to make it impossible to limit group membership to parents with learning difficulties and their partners. Two mothers and a father without learning difficulties were introduced in this way.

- It was not possible to advertise the groups as being for parents in general without attracting people without learning difficulties. Equally, it was not possible to publicise them as being for parents with learning difficulties, because group members would have found the label stigmatising.

- Ideally, it might have been better occasionally to run separate sessions, for example, for fathers or for parents whose children had been removed or for young mothers with babies, but the numbers were never sufficient to permit such a development.

- Although the workers said the parents owned the groups, the parents themselves saw the set-up differently, because the running costs were met elsewhere. This meant that when funding ceased there was no agreement among the parents about how to keep the groups going.

Group processes

- Without taking on a leadership role themselves, workers had to ensure that the more articulate members did not take over the group for their own purposes or to the exclusion of other parents.

- Workers had to find ways of drawing everyone into the meeting in order to ensure that parents did not talk only to them.

- People had to learn how to talk in a group and to respect conventions such as turn-taking in conversation.

Hurting others

- Workers had to stick by the ground rules laid down by the parents, even when this entailed upsetting someone. For example, one mother had to be asked not to bring her teenage son because the group had agreed that only children under five could attend with their parent(s).

- Humour must be handled carefully. Jokes can easily be taken the wrong way, especially by people who are often laughed at or ridiculed.

- Talking about children can be painful to people who have lost theirs.

- It was very easy for people who had suffered a lot of trouble and heartbreak in their lives to be reminded of things they would prefer to forget by casual remarks, the wrong words, or minor squabbles within the group. Anticipating the effects of what was going on in meetings called for constant vigilance and an awareness of people's sensitivities.

- Not everyone got on all the time, and inevitably this fact created tensions that had to be managed in the meetings. Fall-outs sometimes meant that some parents stayed away from the group for a while.

Perceptions

- Learning to be assertive within the group was one thing, but carrying over that learning outside the group proved much more difficult.

- Parents' anger against the system sometimes turned into jealousy of each other when they found they were being treated differently by practitioners or the services.

- It was noticeable that parents were ready to buy presents and birthday cards for the workers, but not for each other.

- The workers recognised their commonality with members as parents, but were aware that their lived experience was far removed from the daily lives of the mothers and fathers in the group.

- The workers had to justify any absence from meetings, otherwise parents thought they had found other more important or interesting things to do.

What the parents gained

Friendship, peer support and caring about others

The groups were a catalyst for bringing parents together, rather than an end in themselves. Some parents stayed in touch between meetings and after the project finished. The parents' feelings for each other showed in countless small ways:

- Mothers helped with the babies and young children during meetings.

- One mother taught another how to use the tram.

- They met up to go shopping together and for evenings out.

- Three mothers started baby-sitting and going round each other's houses.

- Parents brought baby clothes for a new mother.

- They swopped tips and information, like where to find good second-hand equipment.

- They helped each other get to places using public transport.

- They showed concern about each other's problems.

- They grieved with parents who lost their children after court cases.

- They comforted a bereaved mother.

Relaxation

- The group offered parents — especially single mothers — respite from the sole company of their children.

- Some mothers enjoyed having a break from their partner, especially where they were usually cooped up at home together for most of the week.

- The meetings helped to relieve parents' boredom by giving them something different to look forward to and a break in routine.

- Parents enjoyed being with other adults and just having a natter.

A safe place

- Parents found solace in being able to share their feelings with people who had been through the same mill.

- Parents were accepted for who they were and did not have to justify themselves.

- It offered an escape from outside pressures.

- It was somewhere where they were believed.

- It reassured people of their status as parents, especially those whose children had been taken away.

Being responsible and making decisions

- Parents were accountable to the group for what they had agreed to do and for carrying it through.

- Parents learned about living with group decisions.

- The group provided a space for parents where no-one told them what to do.

Feeling equal

- The group provided a forum where parents could address their problems without having to defer to 'experts' or 'power people'.

New learning

- Discussing problems, meeting new people, asking for advice, making complaints, getting information — all helped people develop new skills and qualities, such as:
    - speaking up for themselves
    - knowing when to say sorry

- coping with disagreements
- sharing painful experiences
- trusting others and exchanging confidences
- listening
- enjoying companionship
- considering others' feelings
- looking before leaping
- dealing with anger
- tolerance.

What the parents said about the groups

Stella

'I liked meeting new people and getting on with them. I was always stuck in before. It was a break from the children. I liked the coffee and biscuits at the group.'

Julie

'When you've got young kids it's nice to have a break and get out of house, talk to other parents. It's something to look forward to. It was nice to go. Even just going to McDonald's for a meal with others instead of sitting there alone with three kids. Kids could meet others too. I knew one mum from seeing her at school. We see each other quite a lot now. I can talk to her about anything, better than my family. Like abuse. We talk about things. Not in front of our children, we don't want them to hear. But both of us were abused.'

Dilly

'When I went to nursery, I didn't talk to other people. I just dropped my daughter off and picked her up. Because of group I am able to meet new people and talk with them. I'm more open. With going to that group I found it good. One day at nursery,

I just started talking to Julie and I introduced her to group and she right enjoyed it.'

Tricia

'The group helped me as it got me talking about my anger. When I talked about my daughter it made it seem as if she was there. I met new people and it helped me express my views and it was all confidential. It was good to talk to others, it got rid of some frustrations. It made me feel like a mum. The group helped me talk my problems through. It filled Mondays up for me and was something to look forward to. I made friends. It made me realise that I wasn't on my own, there are others in similar situations.'

Catherine

'Everyone supported each other and we are friends. Getting into the group stopped me looking at four walls. I found the group and having an advocate useful for all the information. I believe the group helped everyone that came. I felt guilty sometimes bringing my son to the group as I knew that Moira and Gillian couldn't bring their children. When a parent is talking in the group, and listening to what they are going through each week, and taking an interest in, and just by talking to new people, you think you're not the only one in the world with problems.'

Emily

'The group helped by supporting me and giving me someone to talk to. It was somewhere to go and it got me out. I didn't like it when people got upset. It's somewhere to meet new people and talk and share problems. I get a lot out of talking to different

*people. Everyone has been good to me.
Thank you all for being there.'*

Eric

'It's somewhere where we can be honest.'

Moira

*'I could talk to others about things we've
gone through, sharing, advice on problems.
I enjoyed doing the leaflets. I supported
Emily when Eric died. I made friends in
the group. I enjoyed meeting people, I liked
the company. I felt safe talking there and
better after talking. The group helped me
by being able to talk about losing Stewart.
The group is different, it's different because
it's nothing to do with services. We sort out
other people's problems. I look forward to
going to group. I don't know what I'll do
when the group finishes. I will miss all my
friends.'*

Gillian

*'The group suits me. It's a really good thing.
I can go when my little girl is at nursery.
If we have any problems, other people can
suggest solutions or we give people advice.
I think that new people will find it hard
to come because they don't know anyone.
Members must think of how to keep it
going ... I want group to continue. We con-
fide in each other. I've enjoyed coming to
Parents Together. Everybody's been there
to listen. I enjoy listening to other parents
and what they've been through. It gets you
away from family pressures, although I
know they're still there. I'm sad it's coming
to an end. We might go to a different group
but it's not going to be the same. It's coming to an end and we're going to be split up
when we don't want to be.'*

Chapter Ten
Conclusions

Parents Together was based on an explicit model of parenting and social support. This model rejects the narrow view equating parental competence with parentcraft. Instead, it holds that the ability of parents to fulfil their responsibilities is also influenced by the environmental pressures bearing on the family and the kind of social support the family receives. Building on this model, **Parents Together** set out to lighten the load on parents by using advocacy:

- to reduce the environmental pressures on parents that undermine their ability to cope

- to challenge discriminatory views of their fitness for parenthood

- to support parents in ways that improve their self-esteem.

This report has outlined the principles which guided the project, described the work of the advocates and drawn out the wider lessons for practice that emerged. The question remaining is how far the advocacy approach was successful in achieving these aims. Our experience of doing the project leads us to the following conclusion:

> The parents felt better for having an advocate, but the advocates could do little to change their situation.

This broad conclusion sums up the project but needs to be filled out.

In terms of the model of support on which the project was based (see p5), **Parents Together** had little success in relieving the environmental pressures on parents, but it did succeed in changing for the better the way in which the parents were regarded by some practitioners and the kind of support they were given.

> Advocacy cannot ameliorate parents' troubles, but it can act to prevent them being compounded by bad practice and competence-inhibiting support.

One-to-one advocacy work with parents who have learning difficulties is like pushing string. The pressures on the parents and the problems they face are unremitting (see *Appendix 3* for a list of the pressures on families recorded over the 18-month span of the project). At the same time, services geared to the needs of these families are missing, and what services there are tend to be crisis-orientated, child-centred rather than family-focused, unreliable, inflexible, uncoordinated and thin on the ground. Consequently, there are few resources available for the advocate to mobilise in order to relieve the environmental strains on parents.

> Advocacy can successfully challenge specific instances of bad practice but it cannot change the system that generates it.

We encountered many examples of good practice by practitioners and recognised that many of them shared the same frustrations in being unable to access appropriate services.

> Without an adequate infrastructure of health and social services, advocacy alone is unable to relieve the environmental pressures that undermine parents' ability to cope.

Discriminatory attitudes among professionals (most notably those without experience of working with people who have learning difficulties) and the public make it harder for an advocate to galvanise action in support of parents, while the scale of the problems the parents face ensures no let-up in their need for advocacy support. This two-pronged source of pressure easily pushes advocates into taking on more than they can realistically hope to manage, with the attendant danger of disillusionment and exit.

Life is tough for parents with learning difficulties. The pressures that bear down on them can weary their advocate, too. An advocate cannot expect to change agency policies or practices that impact unfairly on families, make professionals like the parents or treat them with respect, undo the harm done by deficiencies in the services and support provided to families, shield people from discrimination and day-to-day harassment or change the attitudes that fuel their victimisation in the community. Equally, an advocate cannot erase past hurts or ensure a future free from distress.

> Advocates were no more successful than the parents themselves over the longer term at dealing with the failings in the system. In both cases, individuals were worn down by the constant struggle to get anything done.

Despite these constraints on the advocate's role, **Parents Together** has shown that parents with learning difficulties will continue to receive rough justice and their children a raw deal without some kind of advocacy support to combat the effects of system abuse. However, this conclusion should not divert attention from parents' real needs.

> The goal should be to get the system working better to support families, rather than to get everyone an advocate.

The advocacy support groups were more successful in converting effort into effect. They:

- got to more people for less advocacy time
- allowed parents to meet each other
- served as a platform for challenging discriminatory attitudes
- boosted parents' self-esteem and confidence
- provided opportunities for learning
- brought some fun into people's lives.

> The advocacy support groups were successful in helping people to work with their problems (if not resolve them) and to feel better about themselves.

But not everyone was able or wanted to attend a support group. Even the people who did regularly go along to the groups had some problems that were better addressed, confidentially, on a one-to-one basis.

> Support groups represent an extension of, rather than a substitute for, one-to-one advocacy.

The parents liked the advocates' ways of working. They liked knowing that nothing was being done behind their back; they liked having copies of everything that was written about them; they liked having easy contact with their advocate; they liked being listened to and treated with respect.

> The parents endorsed the practice principles followed by **Parents Together**.

The advocacy approach adopted by **Parents Together** serves as a model of how to work in partnership with parents who have learning difficulties. Indeed, given that many of the factors undermining their ability to cope are the same as those that make it hard for people without learning difficulties to be good parents, the approach has implications for practitioners working in partnership with all families in need.

> The principles and practice points outlined in this report serve as guidelines for all practitioners seeking to work in partnership with families.

Appendix 1

Selected references from the USA on supported parenting

Espe-Sherwindt, M. (1991) The ISFP and parents with special needs/mental retardation. *Topics in Early Childhood Special Education*, **11** (3) 107–120.

Espe-Sherwindt, M. & Crable, S. (1993) Parents with mental retardation: moving beyond the myths. *Topics in Early Childhood Special Education*, **13** (2) 154–174.

Espe-Sherwindt, M. & Kerlin, S. (1990) Early intervention with parents with mental retardation: do we empower or impair? *Infants and Young Children*, **2**, 21–28.

Heighway, S. (1992) *Helping Parents Parent: A practice guide for supporting families headed by parents with cognitive limitations.* Supported Parenting Project. Madison: Wisconsin Council of Developmental Disabilities.

Heighway, S., Kidd-Webster, S. & Snodgrass, P. (1988) Supporting parents with mental retardation. *Children Today*, (November–December) 24–27.

Hoffman, C., Mandeville, H., Webster, S. K., Heighway, S., Ullmer, D., Mincberg, B., Snodgrass, P., Murphy-Simon, K. & Wenger, B. (1990) *The Amelioration of Health Problems of Children with Parents with Mental Retardation 1987–1990.* Madison, Wisconsin, USA: Wisconsin Council on Developmental Disabilities and the Waisman Center on Mental Retardation and Human Development.

Kidd Webster, S. (1988) *Service Delivery to Families in Wisconsin in Which Parents have Mental Retardation.* Madison, Wisconsin: Waisman Center on Mental Retardation and Human Development.

Mandeville, H. (Ed.) (1992a) *Building the Foundation: Public policy issues in supported parenting.* Supported Parenting Project. Madison: Wisconsin Council on Developmental Disabilities.

Mandeville, H. (1992b) Guiding principles for supporting families headed by parents with disabilities. In H. Mandeville (Ed.) *Building the Foundation: Public policy issues in supported parenting.* Supported Parenting Project (pp 5–7). Madison, Wisconsin: Wisconsin Council on Developmental Disabilities.

New York State Commission on Quality of Care for the Mentally Disabled (1993) *Serving Parents who are Mentally Retarded: A review of eight parenting programs in New York State.* New York: New York State Commission on Quality of Care for the Mentally Disabled.

Snodgrass, P. (1992) How many? How much? Scarce resources and supported parenting. In H. Mandeville (Ed.) *Building the Foundation: Public policy issues in supported parenting.*

Supported Parenting Project. Madison, Wisconsin: Council on Developmental Disabilities.

Snodgrass, P. (1993) *What's Wrong With You? An Occasional Paper*, Health Promotion Project, University of Wisconsin-Madison, Madison, Wisconsin.

Tymchuk, A. (1990) *Parents with Mental Retardation: A national strategy*. Paper prepared for the President's Committee on Mental Retardation, SHARE/UCLA Parenting Project, Department of Psychiatry, School of Medicine, University of California at Los Angeles.

Ullmer, D., Kidd Webster, S. & McManus, M. (1991). *Cultivating Competence: Models of support for families headed by parents with cognitive limitations — a national resource directory*. Madison, Wisconsin: Waisman Center on Mental Retardation and Human Development and Wisconsin Council on Developmental Disabilities.

Appendix 2

Sample withdrawal plan

CONFIDENTIAL COPY TO PARENTS

WITHDRAWAL PLAN	*to be discussed and agreed with parents*

NAME(S) OF PARENT(S):   Emily Burgess

Parent(s) view of short-term needs and possible solutions

NEEDS	POSSIBLE SOLUTIONS
new cooker	social worker is checking out
carpets	social worker is checking out
wardrobe	social worker is checking out
new bed for Simon	social worker is checking out
disposing of cat	Emily to phone RSPCA
new hoover	Emily to ask sister to help buy
new settee and storage unit	nephew to supply when he buys replacements for his house

Parent(s) view of ongoing, long-term needs and possible solutions

NEEDS	POSSIBLE SOLUTIONS
bereavement counselling	counsellor contacting Emily – October
college courses	Emily enrolling July for 1997/8
decorating house	awaiting cheque from housing – two nephews to help Jack (elder son)
getting to appointments	Jack and Emily's sister to accompany
learning to cook	support worker to help
learning to shop	support worker to help
managing house (washing/cleaning)	support worker to help
managing own benefits	social worker to help
health – especially teeth and diet	community nurse or social worker
help get Simon to school	education welfare officer
pay-phone in house	social worker to check out

Guidance Note

Plan might include:

- *telling extended family about withdrawal of advocacy support*
- *telling professionals involved about withdrawal of advocacy support*
- *referring parents to other agencies for help with a specific need.*

Appendix 3

Pressures on parents

This appendix lists the source and/or nature of the pressures experienced by parents during the course of the project.

Personal

- poor health, e.g. asthma, epilepsy
- physical/sensory impairments
- restricted mobility
- bereavement
- loss of main carer
- fear of losing children
- loss of child or grandchild through adoption or fostering
- managing time
- keeping appointments
- managing money on a daily basis
- debts and paying large bills
- fear of prison
- difficulties with laundry/cooking/shopping/cleaning/decorating
- mental health problems
- limited reading and writing abilities
- lack of stability – partnership/house
- physical abuse
- rape
- sexual harassment
- verbal abuse
- emotional abuse
- no emotional support
- single parent
- problems with methods of contraception
- fear of another pregnancy
- unexpected pregnancy

Personal history

- sexual abuse/rape in childhood/adulthood
- physical abuse in childhood/adulthood
- unloved in childhood
- witness to abuse of own mother
- own parents separated
- in institution as a child – no family life/no role model
- in hostel as young adult
- special school – segregation/no sex education
- bad memories of living with a partner
- overdosing

Social/economic

- social isolation
- restricted social activities/opportunities
- unemployment
- no break from children
- no holidays
- limited transport
- no use of telephone for emergencies
- furnishing the home
- inadequate housing

- broken domestic appliances
- lack of children's safety equipment (safety-gates and fireguards)

Children

- children's illnesses/health
- children's behaviour
- abusive behaviour of older children
- children in care
- unsatisfactory contact arrangements for children in care
- children's illnesses/injuries when in care
- absenteeism of children from school
- children bullied at school
- infant children in school a long distance away
- older children who contribute nothing to housekeeping
- bedwetting problems
- bedwetting and soiling by children
- children with learning difficulties
- children with physical/sensory impairments
- family size and ages of children

Partner

- violent
- gambling
- heavy drinker
- unemployed
- misuses partner's disability benefit money for own interests
- gives limited support/help in the home
- no financial support from ex-partner
- domestic upheavals
- partnership breakdown
- oppressive male
- mental health problems
- disabled

Extended family

- financial abuse
- ageing parents' health problems
- family trauma – accidents
- poor relationships
- dominating grandparents

Neighbourhood

- financial abuse by friends and wider community
- neighbours asking for money
- neighbours complaining
- harassment by neighbours
- sexually vulnerable to predatory males
- economically vulnerable to door-to-door salesmen/money-lenders
- victims of crime
- fear of being attacked
- victimisation
- nuisance calls
- racism
- vandalism
- discrimination

Practitioners and professionals

- negative attitudes towards parents
- formal meetings where parents cannot articulate feelings
- no practical support when needed
- lack of information
- poor relationships
- involvement too intrusive
- GP dismissive of parent's worries over children

The system

- not knowing how to get things done
- knowing the system but being ignored

- unexplained large bills
- late arrival of giros
- abuse allegations
- criminal proceedings
- inadequate benefits
- rent arrears
- impending court hearings
- postponements of court hearings
- attending core groups/reviews and case conferences

- personal assessments
- attending appeal courts in other towns
- lack of educational opportunities
- bad practice
- finding safe and appropriate housing
- poor inter-agency co-ordination
- benefits inadequate to allow independence.